PRAIS

I Swea

"Deftly written by a dentist who clearly has a winning sense of humor." —Dr. Geoff Jones, VA pediatrician

"Better written than a book I just edited by a best-selling author." —Michael Garrett, Stephen King's first editor

"Amazing stories ... thoroughly enjoyed it!"
—WRWL, Amazon reviewer

"A great tribute to dentistry, family, fellowship, and life."
—Dr. Mary Alice Connor, PA dentist

"Congratulations on telling your interesting story in such a lively way, and mixing in so much history ... I know that's not always easy."
—Steve Vogel, contributor to the *Washington Post*

"A handsome and witty book. A true gem ... can't wait for the sequel." —Cynthia Armstrong, MD, RN

"Couldn't put it down!"
—Bill Rhea, underemployed Texas nice guy

"This book is so funny—I'm glad Dr. James has written another book, *The Whole Tooth*. I just loved it."
—Valerie Townsend

"A heartwarming story that I could not put down."

—Lisa, an Amazon reader

"Very entertaining. I highly recommend it!"

—Amazon customer

"An easy read and very good. I'm looking forward to the next book with baited breath!" —Marsha Braunstein

"This is a very sweet book about normal people, their lives and loves and struggles." —Leslie F.

"I really enjoyed reading *I Swear to Tell the Tooth* and can't wait until the next one is published so I can recommend it to my friends." —Dr. Natalia Tomona

"A delightful read. I loved every minute of it and can't wait for the next one." —Janet R.

I SWEAR TO TELL THE TOOTH

Other books by Dr. Carroll James

The Whole Tooth

I SWEAR TO TELL THE TOOTH

Humorous (and Sometimes Touching) Tales from a Globe-Trotting Dentist's Storied Life

by

DR. CARROLL JAMES

RP
RIDGE PUBLISHING

Second Edition

Published 2016

ISBN: 978-0-9967917-3-1
Library of Congress Control Number: 2016948020

Editing and book design by Stacey Aaronson

Published by:
RidgePublishing

Printed in the United States of America

This book is dedicated to Karen,
my loving soul mate

CONTENTS

PROLOGUE

Terrified, I shoot bolt upright. "Wha' … what's happening?"

It's just a dream, you idiot, a small voice of reason says from a heavy fog deep within my brain.

But why does she come around so often? an urgent cry demands.

I'm ten years old—maybe eight or twelve. *Bonanza* is over and I've just donned my PJs, tired and ready for sleep. It feels good to close my eyes, to picture Hoss Cartwright riding the range, protecting the world from evildoers.

He crests the far ridge to disappear into the vastness of the American West, and a restlessness envelops me. I'm left alone to patrol the range. The echo of pounding hooves fades in the distance; our house becomes almost too quiet. Everyone in my family has fallen asleep, and my mind kicks into overdrive while myriad visions creep in to suffocate me in the darkness. My soul virtually tosses and turns to keep the world spinning in its proper orbit, for which I feel responsible. It's my charge … and my curse.

In the dream, I'm in Grandpa's clapboard farmhouse, nestled against a hill up on The Ridge, being chased by someone who's laughing all the while. It's fun until I round the corner into Grandma's bedroom and suddenly sense that it's not one of my mischievous cousins, or my sometimes diabolical brother, or even my crazy, senile grandfather. I catch a glimpse of a pointed black hat (and no one in my family wears pointed black hats). And it's not really a person—of that I'm sure.

The laughing abruptly stops, and I duck into the only closet in the old farmhouse, one of those musty old closets that only has hooks along its shallow back wall. I can barely squeeze inside, and with the door closed, it's darker than the black of a moonless Appalachian night with coyotes howling in the near distance.

Then it happens. My muscles tense as the witch throws open the closet door. Although shorter than me, she looms larger in my mind, and hellishly ugly. Her mouth opens wide, spewing breath that reeks of death and howls an evil that seems to emanate from the pit of hell. She lunges at me while her tongue rolls across jagged, scum-covered teeth. My heart pounds like a sledgehammer and I quiver uncontrollably.

Suddenly, I awake in a cold night sweat and find myself sitting upright on drenched sheets in my bed in Maryland, terrified of lying down again to close my eyes.

The dream—the nightmare—followed me from childhood, through adolescence, and into adulthood. It wouldn't let go. The nightmarish images, more vivid than reality, swirled like black-cloaked specters through my mind and pierced my soul. Did it foreshadow my life? Maybe ... probably.

It's sheer terror, the devil's work.

So ... I decide to become a dentist.

CHAPTER ONE

The Decision

Is fear of dentists inherent in our DNA? In the movie *Marathon Man*, where a sadistic Nazi tooth carpenter inflicts horrifying pain, there were more audience groans and screams than in most slasher flicks.

"No offense, Doc. Don't take it personally, but I hate the dentist." I've heard that a hundred, if not a thousand times, and after a while, it gets kinda hard to brush off.

So why choose medical dentistry as a career?

I was scientifically inclined as a kid. I enjoyed building models and excelled academically. I once considered an appointment to the naval academy, but that was before I attended a military high school, bunking with five other guys in a room designed for two. The first night I went to bed homesick, only to be awakened by a clanging bell and the boom of a cannon that shook the old barracks' ancient windows. A bugler then screeched reveille as the OD (Officer of the Day) burst in and whacked my slow-to-get-up bunkmate with the side of his sword. Fifteen minutes later, a quick morning inspection was followed immediately by company formation on the quad before marching off to breakfast and then work detail.

Despite quickly growing weary of that life, I persevered through graduation.

My father constantly traveled for work, so we almost never took a vacation. But during the summer of my sophomore year, Mom talked him into a trip to Niagara Falls. After several heated discussions, he acquiesced—only if the trip could be combined with a business meeting in Buffalo so he could get the company to pay for it. (I was admittedly disappointed to never see a roving Buffalo there.)

From Niagara, it was on to Watkins Glen, where a delightful friend of Mom's had retired to a houseboat. While we relaxed lakeside, the friend suggested that a youngster such as I might do well to consider a career in dentistry. "They don't work very hard and they make a lot of money," she said.

My ears perked up. Soaking up the sunshine, I closed my eyes and pictured my childhood dentist bounding into the hygiene room for his cameo appearance after the pretty hygienist had done all the *real work*. "How are things today, Carroll?" he'd ask as he plunged his fingers into my mouth. Before I could answer, he'd robotically mutter, "Fine, fine." After poking around some, he'd declare, "Well, things look pretty good ... only four cavities. We'll just fill 'em up and see you again in six months. Now be sure to brush *every* day."

Dad, who sported a full set of dentures, thought six-month checkups were just shy of highway robbery. "I'd like to sell shoe inserts to the same lady twice a year," he'd say.

But after hearing what the woman on the houseboat said, I figured I couldn't lose if I set my sights on becoming a dentist.

On the way home, we swung by Lansing, Michigan, which was not really on the way, to fetch my grandmother from Aunt Aida's house.

Grandma had lived her entire life in the hills of southwestern Virginia, born and raised deep inside the magnificently wild, beautiful, and poverty-stricken Appalachian backcountry. After

Grandpa died she sold their ancient farm, which produced little more than rocks, and went to stay with her adult children, and occasionally with her much younger siblings—nine of them, all girls.

The time had come for her to live with us for a spell and I was looking forward to it. She was my favorite grandparent, despite that witch lurking in the dark of her house.

After learning she had a grandson who wanted to be a doctor, that was all Grandma and Mom talked about on the long ride back to Maryland. Grandma was especially enthusiastic. "Can you believe it, Gaye, honey? Carroll's gonna be a doctor!"

Mom echoed her, "A professional in the family. Just think on that!"

Dad mumbled something about four years of college tuition; he didn't know it required eight. Born in 1899, he was quite a bit older than Mom and had never completed high school. As a self-made man, he had little use for "higher larnin'."

As I rode in the back of Dad's Buick, his pride and joy, I'd never seen him drive so fast—it was almost as if he was trying to outrun the nonstop chatter emanating from the backseat, which Mom and Grandma shared alone. My brother, Lee, sat up front in the middle of the bench seat while I rode shotgun. I was a bit frightened at our increased rate of travel, but Lee, grinning all the while, enjoyed it whenever Dad speeded.

Safely back in Maryland, Grandma settled into the spare bedroom next to mine. After a hard life of struggling to make ends meet, she looked much older than her sixty-four years. But a certain radiance, coupled with an ever-so-slight smile, brightened Grandma's withered face every time I mentioned college and dental school.

She loved spending time with her grandsons (the fact that there were no granddaughters was a welcome treat after having nine sisters). Lee and I would sit in her room, mesmerized by endless stories of "them ole days up on The Ridge." She enthusiastically related her favorite memories: when electricity came to Nealy Ridge, the day the first car made it up the treacherous mountainside, when her only telephone was installed (I actually remember when they put in the party line), coal mine cave-ins, and my favorite, rough-and-tumble altercations between *revenuers* and *moonshiners* as federal tax men searched for stills hidden in the dark recesses of the craggy mountains. I envisioned bloodhounds howling, feds shouting, branches breaking, and echoing gunshots before axes smashed into a wood-fired still, spilling white lightening onto the dirt.

On one crisp, yet sunny fall morning while I was getting ready for school, Mom called out, "Carroll! Go fetch yer Grandma. Breakfast is about ready."

I knocked on her bedroom door, but there was no answer. Gently pushing it open, I softly asked, "Grandma. You up?"

The room was dark and eerily cold. Her chamber felt of death, and I knew before I looked. Thankfully her eyes were closed—had they been open, she would've been gazing heavenward. Grandma had died peacefully in her sleep, in the bosom of her family. She's buried next to Grandpa up on The Ridge.

CHAPTER TWO

Beginnings

The tumultuous sixties had come to a close by August of 1971, while the Vietnam War slowly stumbled toward an unresolved conclusion. After four years of premed, I arrived at Farleigh Dickenson University in northern New Jersey along with a herd of other professional wannabes. Most were from the parochial Northeast; in undergrad we'd all been at the tops of our classes—the elite. That, however, would change during the rigors of dental school.

At orientation, I became friends with a few guys with whom I grew closer under the ongoing pressures of professional school.

Stan-the-Man was straitlaced and clean-shaven. With his short-cropped hair, black plastic-rimmed glasses, neatly pressed slacks, starched button-down collar, white socks, and penny loafers, he'd emerged straight from the Buddy Holly fifties, completely bypassing the uniform of the day: bell-bottoms, sandals, and tie-dye T-shirts. Oddly, his arms refused to swing when he walked, which gave him a dorky, robotic gait and made him easy to pick out in a crowd. Stan had spent that hot summer canvassing the urban landscape as a Listerine salesman and was quite adept at selling mouthwash to dentists, which foreshadowed his later success.

In decided contrast, goofy Gill sported the requisite beard, wire-rim glasses, and confident strut of the early seventies. When the school cited an obscure study about facial hair breeding harmful bacteria and pressured anyone with a beard to shave, Gill's wife recorded the traumatic sheering on silent 8mm film. I couldn't hear him weep, but I think a tear trailed down his bare face.

Rock was rebel-lite, like The Fonz on *Happy Days*, an unabashed free spirit. But unlike Fonzie, Rock already showed signs of male pattern baldness, which he accentuated by growing his stringy hair extremely long, halfway down his back. Rather than garnering grief about hitch-hiking bacteria, he carefully rolled and secured his mane with bobby pins, which gave his sparsely covered pate a monastic appearance. By day, he looked the part of a mild-mannered dentist, except for one thing—the school's dress code was a white lab coat over a dress shirt, slacks, and tie, but they forgot to specify what kind of neckwear was appropriate. Rock's only tie made psychedelic seem tame. (Every morning, rain or shine, Rock rode a BMW muscle bike to school. When heading home one evening, he removed the hairpins, and with no confining helmet to tame his thinning locks, they trailed freely in the wind. He took the narrow, winding mountain roads in northwest Jersey much too fast and once missed a curve, launching himself handlebar deep into Lake Lackawanna. Rock replaced the ruined BMW with a tricked-out Harley.)

The lovably rotund Floyd exuded an unkempt aura, like Pig Pen of Peanuts. When we hung out at the Jersey Shore, Floyd had the whitest body on the beach. In order to burn evenly, he'd roll over in slow motion until his chubby body was bright red. "You look like a beached whale," Rock said. Floyd merely glanced up from his dime novel and with his sharp wit said with a wry grin, "Leave me alone. I'm protected by Greenpeace." Although no babe magnet, he did marry and later sired twins, which was ironic because Floyd had only one testicle.

Me? I sort of fit somewhere in the middle of these chums. When not in my regulation school clothes, I donned jeans or summer cutoffs, flannels or T-shirts, and I shaved my college beard before Labor Day. My mild southern accent and down-home colloquialisms elicited grins and comments from my newfound northern friends about my "hick roots." I considered nurturing this persona by wearing Grandpa's string tie, but then thought better of it. Overall, my buddies treated me like a mascot, as if I were from the planet Zork.

As women were just beginning to realize a long overdue equality in the American workplace, only five graced our class of seventy-five freshmen, none of whom made it into our little clique of gents.

Four of those five ladies were ordinary folk, like everyone else.

The fifth was not.

Ms. Oleander Jacob's personal hygiene was nothing short of foul—or nonexistent—her body odor always warning us of her approach. She outdid Floyd on the gross meter, but even he was too affable to be disgusting. Oleander's uniform of a frayed-wool poodle skirt and a heavy plaid vest didn't scream stylish, especially paired with combat-like boots and dull white knee socks. It's a miracle she survived the last heat wave of summer.

In lab class, we were assigned seats alphabetically, like in grade school, so Ms. Jacob ended up next to me for clinical training over the four long years of dental school. Unfortunately, she lacked the "hands" (i.e., manual dexterity) to perform excellent, good, or even marginal dentistry, and when students were paired with one another for clinical exercises, I was inevitably yoked with "twitchy fingers," squirming in pain every time she practiced a new procedure on me. Being her personal guinea pig for prophys ("cleanings" in dental speak) was the worst.

"You're digging into my gums," I would say while she stripped off the top layer.

"They're all red. You have periodontitis," she would say defensively.

I don't have gum disease; they're red because you're hacking at them.

"I taste blood."

"Let me try again," she would insist.

It would take a week for my gums to recover.

One of the joys (ha ha) of dental school was taking "practicals"—clinical tests using plastic mouths—which carried a strict time limit and zero tolerance for inaccuracies. One such exam tested our didactic skills by having us fabricate a wax crown, or cap, on a plaster die we'd made previously. In private practice, that's usually a job for the dental lab, but we had to execute (poor choice of words?) every step of the process ourselves.

Understandably tense and jittery in approaching the cap-carving test, the students had to soften the wax over an open flame and shape it with heated instruments. The simplest mistake could be a major setback, leading to total failure. One instructor called practicals "sweaty palm time," but prospective doctors needed to become accustomed to the pressures of private practice, so into the fire we went.

It was unusually quiet as we filed into the bright lab to arrange our instruments on stainless-steel countertops that gleamed in the fluorescent glare. Drawers and cabinets were yanked open, riffled through, and slammed shut while tense whispers drifted heavily through the sterile air.

"I've misplaced my wax instrument. Does anyone have an extra one?"

"I need a match. Anybody got one? How 'bout a lighter?"

"Nobody smokes in here you nimrod."

"I'll bet Rock can scrounge one up. He smokes. Well, not cigarettes."

"Gotta fire up the butane somehow. Hey, wait a minute. I can't find my Bunsen burner. Anybody seen it?"

A trace of desperation permeated the room as the stern proctor distributed a block of inlay wax, color coded so no one could sneak in a preformed crown, to each future dentist. Hearts pounded as the gymnasium-style wall clock's minute hand clicked north, waiting for the instructor to commence the test with a solemn, "Now!"

Everyone buckled down to the task at hand; sulfur from striking matches wafted through the air as the distinct *woof* of gas burners announced they were ablaze. Oleander, seated immediately to my left, was more grimy-greasy-gross than usual, and her odor mingled with the scent of cheap candles and the stifling heat of seventy-five miniature campfires. The mix weighed ponderously in the air, making the tension seem ever more onerous.

But then, a familiar stench passed by. Several nearby students looked up, sniffing the air like basset hounds.

Burning hair!

My head instinctively snapped left in time to witness the top of Ms. Jacob's head burst forth in fiery glory. With mouth agape, I managed to stammer quietly, "Oleander, you ... you ... your hair is on fire!"

Showing no alarm, she swatted absentmindedly at her head, as one might at an annoying fly. Then, irritated by the interruption, she briefly glared at me before bending over the lab bench again, her chin pressed firmly against her chest to peer through her coke-bottle eyeglasses.

After all, the clock was ticking.

But not only had she failed to extinguish the blaze, her flailing had further fanned the flames, which continued to creep across her oily mop. Floyd, who sat to Oleander's immediate left, also noticed the flames and sprang into action. He grabbed a stack of paper towels from the back sink and ran them under the faucet, then, firmly clutching the wet wad, he dashed back to his seat and smacked her head. His heroics, however, merely created a breeze that encouraged the flames to further reach heavenward. Maybe it was my imagination, but I thought I saw a hint of blue. Was the conflagration going critical?

Maybe that student who couldn't find a burner could use Oleander's head, I thought.

Throughout it all, Ms. Jacob continued to work diligently, her detached countenance in direct contrast to the flames shooting ever higher. Floyd and I had to do something to extinguish that blaze, but water to douse it wouldn't answer with all that grease lurking in the depths of her disheveled locks. Baking soda wasn't readily available, and the fire extinguisher seemed inappropriate. (Then again, that might have been fun.)

Short on options, I jumped up, knocking my stool over in the process. The steel crashed to the floor with a loud clang, which caught the attention of an ever-growing radius of students gazing wide-eyed at the pyrotechnic glory of Oleander, the Human Torch. After filling a rubber mixing bowl with tap water, I flung it on her head. Miraculously, the flames immediately died.

But Oleander was drenched.

You might think she would've been grateful, or even possibly angry that I'd soaked her to the skin. But she simply kept on working, never again raising her chin from her chest.

The instructor kept vigil by reading a cheap paperback and only briefly glanced up at the sound of my reverberating stool, somehow still clueless. The students in the immediate vicinity of our little bonfire glanced around and grinned, enjoying the comic relief, while those seated further from the epicenter remained unaware, diligently carving their paraffin cubes without so much as pausing to see where the stench had come from.

With the cranial fire snuffed, Oleander, along with the entire class, was safe from immediate harm, but it was now difficult for those of us directly involved to concentrate. Furtively making eye contact, we quietly chuckled through half smiles. From time to time the proctor put his book down and strolled around to inspect our progress, never suspecting there'd been a close call in the "J" section.

Everyone managed to pass that test, including Ms. Jacob, who never acknowledged our help in rescuing her from a fiery death. The following day she arrived at school as slimy as ever, not even having taken the time to wash her hair—forever true to form. When she wasn't looking, I discreetly searched for a burnt spot on her scalp but couldn't see one. Somehow, the scorched area simply blended in. She looked up, caught me staring and actually smiled. I weakly smiled back, praying that I wasn't sending the wrong signal.

CHAPTER THREE

Homer

Cadaver: *n.* Latin: from *cadere,* to fall. A corpse, as for dissection; a dead body, especially of a person. From: *Webster's Unabridged Dictionary.*

24/7 Homer: *n.* English: from cadaver, stiff, morgue meat. A Freshman's constant companion. From: *The School of Dental Medicine.*

How much information can be stuffed into the human brain? Take a wild guess, double it, and that's what you're expected to learn during dental school. The first two of four years covers the basic sciences, the first big hurdle being Human Anatomy.

Cat anatomy in undergrad helped me prepare. For a whole semester I toted a formaldehyde-saturated, half-butchered specimen across campus that was stuffed in a clear plastic bag (the see-through bag was a nice touch by some instructor with a sick sense of humor). I spent hours in my Gettysburg frat house—to the constant protesting of my AXP brothers—hovering over a dead cat sprawled on newspaper on the library table. Despite the long hours, I enjoyed comparative anatomy and looked forward to human dissection in dental school.

To get our feet wet, we first studied osteology—bones—where four students gathered around sixteen stainless-steel tables, on each of which lay a disarticulated human skeleton, the ultimate 3D puzzle.

Tediously, we aligned each piece and memorized its physical properties: ligament and tendon attachments, grooves for blood vessels and nerves, cartilage articulations, load characteristics, etc., in preparation for dissecting a real human being. Well, a real *dead* one anyway.

At the end of six weeks, there was a practical exam, where attached tags indicated the bone, or part of a bone, to be identified. When the proctor's bell rang, students shuffled to the next table after recording their answer—not much fun at eight in the morning after pulling an all-nighter. Needless to say, coffee was a dental student's constant companion.

One Monday morning, everyone was excited about the sixteen fresh stiffs that were due in. I stopped in the lounge for my quintessential cup of high-test before catching the elevator to the second floor. When the door opened, the stench of formaldehyde overpowered the comforting aroma of my java. *Yep, this is the day of the dead.* When I pulled open the heavy lab door, my eyes watered as the scent hit me even harder. But through the tears, I saw that the dissection table's steel hoods, like on a backyard grill, were closed.

"Don't open them yet," announced the humorless mortician we'd nicknamed Mort. "I want to go over a few do's and don'ts."

Mort proceeded to drone on about the proper etiquette for slicing and dicing the deceased, reminding us that "these people are just like you and me."

Rock snuck a quick peak under his hood. "They're not *exactly* like us," he said with a whisper and a grin.

Mort glanced in Rock's general direction but continued. "Many donated their bodies to science. Others were homeless. Despite the circumstances of their demise, they all demand proper respect." Mort's monotone was sobering, especially his final admonition. "Anyone behaving inappropriately or making distasteful jokes will be asked to leave."

That got our attention. Being kicked out of lab, even for a day, would be a serious setback. You can't really stuff a cadaver into a clear plastic bag and drag it back to your apartment for study.

Continuing his Ben Stein-like cadence (remember *Ferris Bueller's Day Off*?), Mort announced, "You may now open the hoods and retrieve your dissection trays from the middle drawers."

The tops swooshed open to a chorus of gags and gasps. Oddly enough, I wasn't overly affected, probably inured to death by the shoutn'-'n-wailn' during the Nealy Ridge funerals of my youth—not to mention that the lab setting paled in comparison to finding my beloved grandmother deceased in her bed.

After dabbing my eyes, which were tearing to ward off the formaldehyde, I noticed that the cadavers appeared something less than human, almost plastic, especially with their shaved heads and lack of clothes. But despite that, I did immediately determine that mine was a male.

The chief of human anatomy, who supposedly hailed from Argentina, strode into the lab and announced, "Ve vill start vit' ze scalp." It seemed doubtful that South America was his fatherland. "Please turn page t'ree of ze dissection manual."

Edgar Allen Poe couldn't have accentuated the macabre any better.

Dissecting the scalp by carefully peeling back the cranial skin took about an hour or so, which wasn't too bad. There's not much underneath except bone, and all of the students were familiar with that.

But heading south was a whole different story. A person's face gives him identity, and cutting into it seemed like an invasion of his humanity. My stomach turned. I glanced around and saw that Stan and Gill were equally squeamish, having looked away from their respective tables.

This four-hour session was repeated three times a week for the remainder of the year. (For the first full month I couldn't eat meat, but given enough time, you can get used to anything.) And it gradually became clear why Mort had hammered the rules—one way to acclimate to that situation was to dehumanize it. And while we abided by the code of conduct for the most part, we tried to lighten the mood by naming the cadavers. Vinny, a member of my team who hailed from Long island, dubbed ours Homer.

"Homer?" I asked.

"Gotta call 'im something," Vinny declared.

"Yeah. But why Homer?"

"Why da hell not?"

Homer he was christened and Homer he remained. Actually, his full name became 24/7 Homer in honor of the amount of time we seemed to spend with him. Only once have I spent that much time with another person. That was on my honeymoon—but that didn't last a full year.

Pop quizzes became routine. Straining to read tags tied to chunks of an increasingly desecrated body—while racing Mort's timer after getting a good three hours' sleep the previous night—became normal. During the quiz, half the class rotated through the room full of cadavers while the other half was sequestered in an oversized storeroom to await their turn. Wall-to-wall containers held various human parts, and anxious students rummaged through the jugs and cabinets despite Mort's admonition "not to touch anything." His personal stash was forbidden fruit, so we naturally wanted to pluck it.

Leaning sleepy-eyed against a fifty-five gallon drum in the corner, I inadvertently jostled the lid, which slid but didn't topple off. I breathed a sigh of relief, but when Gill further lifted the steel cover to investigate, he lost his grip and it hit the tile floor with a clatter loud enough to wake the dead—and there were quite a few right next door.

Floating atop a thick liquid was one of Mort's weirder collections: bobbing eyeballs that stared lazy-eyed, cross-eyed, and every which way.

"What the hell," Rock grinned.

"Why does Mort keep a can full of enucleated eyes?" Floyd wondered aloud. There must've been hundreds in the drum.

I was trying to make sense of it when the door flew open and Mort beckoned. "You guys are next," he said, stuffing a crème-filled donut into his mouth while Gill discretely replaced the lid.

As weeks progressed into months, the cadavers looked less human, which made the practicals ever more difficult.

"Was that thing on table four part of a liver?"

"Looked more like a slice of pancreas."

"It wasn't brain. Mort put all of them into jars yesterday."

"Gross."

"And the eyeballs were removed from the storeroom," Rock said, sounding disappointed.

As winter gave way to spring, the intensity of freshman year was wearing on everyone, and the young, energetic students of autumn now dragged around in a fog. To finish up the year, a major anatomy practical was scheduled that would decide whether or not we remained in school.

Everyone stayed up the night before to study—and it showed. Disheveled and disoriented, we drifted up to the second floor as if headed to our execution. Even the ladies hadn't bothered to primp. Oleander looked pretty much the same.

I smiled when I stopped at the first table. The Achilles tendon is nicknamed the "freshman ligament" because it's often misidentified. But I knew it, which renewed my confidence. When the buzzer rang, I robotically moved through the familiar routine, but after several stations, sleep deprivation began to take hold.

At the sixth or seventh table, however, I was jarred awake. The steel slab held a middle-aged woman with a full head of slightly gray hair. Only a small incision on the lower border of her right jaw marred her otherwise once-handsome features. With her body covered by a surgical barrier, she seemed merely asleep ... and maybe a little cold.

I stared for the longest time, until my introspective musings were suddenly interrupted by the pierce of Mort's timer. I hadn't even looked at the tag; Rock was already shoving me aside.

The one question I got wrong on that test was on the jaw, with which I should've been most familiar.

I later found out that the woman was assigned to a graduate student who'd only begun dissecting her. Why her hair hadn't been shaved and why her skin didn't have that pasty plastic appearance remained a mystery. At lunch, everyone was talking about her.

"That lady looked so real."

"They're all real, you idiot."

"What say we sneak into the lab tonight and check her out?" someone suggested.

But we never did.

In our junior year, the pathology and anatomy departments collaborated—or conspired—on hospital rotations, and Floyd, Gill, Stan, and I were assigned to assist the pathologist with autopsies at Belmopan Hospital on Manhattan's Lower East Side.

As with most hospitals, the dead were tucked away in the basement. We hopped a crowded elevator and Gill pressed B-4. After riding the creaky old lift down four levels, we immediately stopped in the corridor to gawk at a line of the recently deceased—they lay face up on gurneys, as if waiting to board the next boat across the river Styx, while harried hospital employees rushed past without a glance. Then, Floyd discovered a nondescript door about halfway down the hallway. "I think we're supposed to go in here."

Autopsy/Pathology Room B404

"We're late," Gill said to light a fire under us. "Let's go."

"I don't think the stiffs are going anywhere," Rock said with a smirk.

The door creaked as it opened to a fetid odor that made us gasp. The smell was infused with more than disinfectants or formaldehyde, though they were present in abundance. No, this was more like excrement, sweat, and … dust?

A hospital morgue usually has only two or maybe three autopsy slabs. Not Belmopan. Stiflingly hot and crammed with people, most of them alive and sweating profusely, the room boasted two rows of twelve tables each, jammed into a space designed for about ten. All were occupied and attended by pathologists. Those corpses in the corridor would have to wait for a free table.

The sound of circular saws whirred above the general din as a short doc climbed onto a makeshift step stool and gripped a fat bone saw with both hands to remove the top half of a cranium. Homer's dissection had been more delicate with the small hacksaw-looking thing we'd been issued during freshman year, but here, with twenty-four bodies in the room, at least one or two pathologists were grinding away on skulls at all times, working their way down the row.

Despite their nonchalant demeanor—munching on donuts or bagels while making incisions, which helped me settle in to the surreal scene—I could never bring myself to eat lunch in the hospital's cafeteria.

As part of our learning process, the docs asked us to consider the possible cause of death from only the gross evidence. The guy with half his head blown off in a botched gas station robbery was a no-brainer; we all got that one right.

I was absorbed in one case when Gill tapped my shoulder.

"Carroll. You've got to come with me. A baby, just a few months old, aspirated milk. C'mon, the autopsy is just starting."

He seemed excited but my stomach turned. *There's a baby in this bedlam?* I couldn't wrap my mind around it. *And what about the grieving family?* "That's okay," I said, "I'm plenty busy watching this."

Gill hurried off as I turned back to watch a doc remove a liver at my station. But then I couldn't help myself: I glanced down the line of slabs to see a tiny body, the pinkness of new life replaced by a gray pallor, on a large, cold table. The law demanded an autopsy to rule out foul play. Fair enough, but it was more than I could handle, especially with the birth of my own son eminent. Tears filled my eyes as I looked away.

Each day in the morgue lasted twelve brutal hours that drained us physically and emotionally—but that first day seemed especially long. As we headed past the parade of bodies on our way out, a gurney rolled by with an older man on it, a knife wound tracing a grotesque line across his neck.

If that wasn't enough, a loud commotion began in the adjacent stairwell just as Stan pushed the elevator button. Through the door's window, we saw security guards restraining a middle-aged couple. The woman wailed uncontrollably while she and her husband struggled with the guards. "We just want to see our daughter," the father said with a desperate shout.

"I'm sorry, sir," said the guard, trying to be sympathetic.

"Sorry, my ass. Let us see our little girl."

Apparently their teenager had died of a heart attack while watching TV and was rushed there for a definitive diagnosis. Her parents, their faces contorted in anguish, simply wanted to be by her side. But the rules kept them away, which was a good thing; that was no place to say good-bye to a loved one.

After riding the elevator up and walking past the crowded desks in the lobby, I bumped into a young mother with dark rings around reddened eyes. She was filling out forms for her baby who'd died of aspiration. The poor woman looked numb.

As the four of us hopped into my old, beat-up Ford Falcon, I wrestled with my emotions. We made the hour-and-a-half ride back to Hackensack, New Jersey, in total silence.

As a welcome (well, sometimes) change from the cadavers, we began to treat dental patients—living ones—in our junior year. People actually sign up to endure the long, multiple appointments because the cost is nominal and the work is excellent, being closely monitored by some of the country's best practitioners. But it can take up to nine—that's *nine*—hours, over three sessions, for a student to complete his first filling. I felt pretty good about my first one, which only took six hours over two sessions.

Although the patients knew, more or less, what they were getting into, even the most understanding people got antsy when trapped in a dental chair. Uptight parents trying to save a few bucks were especially aggravating for us to deal with.

Feeling confident after my first treatment, I greeted my second patient, a pleasant high school girl. But I quickly discovered that her father was a most unlikable sort. Slovenly dressed, with a three-day-old beard that wasn't yet stylish, he announced, "Do wha' ya gotta do, Doc. She don't 'preciate nothin' no how."

Ignorant rednecks in Joisey? Who knew?

I dreaded the moment when I had to tell him that she'd have to come back for me to finish.

"Whaddaya mean? How the hell long is this gonna take?"

"I don't know, Mr. Sorrento. It depends on the instructor and how busy we are. You see, each step needs to be checked off and—"

"Jus' git it done quick like. No 'scuses, son." Note that *Doc* had been replaced with a rather condescending *son.* I felt sorry for his daughter, who cringed and sank slump-shouldered into the chair.

Before her second visit, I privately approached the instructor to explain the need to finish the case ASAP. "Is there any way I can get this checked off today?" I asked.

Big mistake.

Graduate professors are not known for their indulgence, and he eyeballed me sideways as he sauntered over to my dental chair in the middle of the large, open clinic.

"Shave about one-tenth of a millimeter off here and then we'll talk, Mr. James."

The old codger shuffled away as a line of students trailed in his wake—like little ducklings waiting for his approval of their work. Before he was again available, the clinic closed, so I had no choice but to place another temporary filling. My second restoration would take the proverbial nine hours. *Why on this yokel's kid?*

"Yer kiddin'? Look, I don't have time for this crap," Mr. Sorrento bellowed. "Her mamma's gonna have ta bring this sorry ingrate back. You be sure ta finish up next time or you got me to answer to."

Mamma has got be better than Dad, I thought.

I was wrong.

When the mother showed up, I quickly discovered that she was even coarser than the unsympathetic father. *Poor kid.* School policy required a guardian to accompany a minor, but this lady wasn't about to stick around. She abandoned her teenage daughter as soon as I began to work on her.

"Her dad will be back later ta pick her up. I don't wanna fool wit' the little bitch. Eighteen won't come soon enough."

Dad showed up at the end, making a ruckus all the while. "Where's that little brat? How come she ain't waitin' fer me out front like I said?"

I had finished early, mainly because a more compassionate

instructor was on duty. "She went to the lounge for a snack, Mr. Sorrento. I'll show you where that is."

"Make it quick. I got better things ta do than chase her sorry ass all around Bergen County," he said with a growl.

The poor girl looked mortified and quickly averted her eyes when he charged into the student lounge. "What the hell you doin' eatin' outta these expensive machines? We ain't made a money, ya know."

You would've thought she'd just purchased a steak at Delmonico's. When he turned and stalked off, she started to follow but then stopped and timidly raised her head.

"Thank you very much," she said to me with a whisper.

"You're welcome. You were a great patient."

She forced a slight smile before hurrying after her father. This young girl had potential in life; she certainly knew how to be appreciative. But her parents seemed determined to squash it before she could blossom. What a shame, a waste.

My mind drifted back to the genuine grief that overflowed from that stark stairwell in the depths of Belmopan Hospital. Those parents of the daughter who had died of a heart attack had a valid reason to make a scene. The lifeless infant lying on the sterile table loomed large in my mind, its poor mother in shock and disbelief.

If only the Sorrentos knew how blessed they were to have a child who was alive and well.

CHAPTER FOUR

Kate Learns to Assist

Dad stared menacingly at me. "Why don't you get a job?" Nervous about the old man's continuing admonitions, I remained frozen to the kitchen chair.

Dad was a large man, still standing tall in his seventies. His dark hair was slicked back, accentuating his J. Edgar Hoover widow's peak. With no formal education beyond sixth grade, he felt that I'd been goofing off during my eight years of college and professional school.

"Even though I've graduated," I said, "I still need a license to practice."

"Humph," he grumbled before storming off, slowly shaking his bulldog head.

The summer of '75 dragged into its second month. At first I'd relished the free time, especially with my kids Tara and Russell. But they were often out with new friends or with their mom. After the rigors of dental school, their mother and I had grown apart. We decided to separate, which ultimately led to divorce.

Now it was just me, lazing around my parents' house all

day. I began to think Dad might be right, but what was I to do without a permit to legally practice dentistry?

I spent a lot of time pacing. When I stopped circling and sat down to stare out the window, my leg began to jerk like a jackhammer. *Will I ever hear from the state board?* I wondered.

Between pacing sessions, I'd sent out dozens of job feelers but no one wanted an unlicensed dentist. Dad continued to believe I was freeloading, but on a hot, muggy day in the month of despair, I saw the postman put a large envelope in our mailbox.

I dashed down the driveway. "Whoa there, Carroll. Looking for something?" he asked.

"Yes, sir, maybe that brown folder you just stuffed in there."

He pulled it back out and looked. "It's from the Maryland Board of Dental Examiners."

"Thank you, Mr. Cooley," I said, frantically tearing it open and reading the cover letter: "Congratulations Dr. James. You have successfully passed the Northeast Regional Board examinations."

I smiled until I read further: "Your records will be transferred shortly."

Shortly? I needed those transcripts before taking the required jurisprudence exam.

When the records finally arrived a week later, I hand-delivered them to a nice secretary in Baltimore who allowed me to take the law test that day. I passed with one hundred percent but still had to wait for the final paperwork to be processed. In the meantime, I had a family to support and my father's patience had about run out.

It seemed like a year before another oversized brown envelope finally arrived holding a certificate embossed in gold lettering: **Carroll James, DMD.**

My career could finally begin.

One of the dentists I'd contacted on the phone practiced in Rockville. Although I had never met him and hadn't told him I was now available. Dr. Rolph Dolph called the very next day to offer me an associateship.

"Why don't you come in and look things over?" he said, "see if you like my office."

I already liked it. "Uh … yeah … great! When's a good time?"

"How 'bout tomorrow, say around five? And what kind of name is Carroll, anyway? Thought you were a girl."

He didn't remember our earlier conversation.

"Family name," I muttered. I'd been self-conscious about my name as a kid, but the name wasn't all that unusual. Actor Carroll O'Connor made it work for him; so did my maternal uncle and namesake. I wanted to shout, "There's a Carroll County in Maryland." But I didn't. I just wanted a job.

Dr. Dolph's ground floor office was located in an upscale apartment building. A mahogany door led from the main hall into a dimly lit waiting room with a high ceiling. The walnut paneled walls were lined with brown leather furniture that sat on plush carpeting, and heavy drapes covered the floor-to-ceiling window. It had the feel of a Victorian library. Being a bookworm, I was impressed.

But I was more enamored by the buxom receptionist, immodestly attired in a low-cut blouse and tight chinos. Her perfectly straight, very white teeth—probably caps—brightened the dark room when she smiled. She moved like a Playboy Bunny, which I found out later she once was. "Can I help you?" she asked while leaning across the reception counter, cleavage first.

Flustered, I tried to look away. "Uh … I'm here to see Dr. … uh … Dr. Dolph."

"We're closing for the day." Her toothy smile faded to fake. *Maybe like her chest?*

"Oh, I'm not here for an appointment. Well … I guess I am. It's just that I'm looking for a job and …"

"Wait here," she said, interrupting me as her smile disappeared.

Real smooth, Carroll. I'd been there only a few minutes and had already alienated Dr. Dolph's pretty receptionist, who simply wanted to go home after a long day's work. My palms felt clammy when he burst through the back door and exclaimed, "Good to meet you, Carl."

"It's Carro ... Uh, nice to meet you, too," I stammered.

His overly tight tunic accentuated bulging muscles, and his firm grasp squeezed the wet from my hand, like wringing a dishrag. I wondered if I'd left a puddle on the floor.

A cursory tour revealed the lack of assistant stools, high-speed suction, and air-water syringes. In fact, the old office lacked any ergonomic design for modern, sit-down, four-handed dentistry. Elderly dentists could be easily spotted in a crowd, shuffling along and hunched over like Quasimodo.

But despite his antiquated office, Dr. Dolph ran a dental maintenance organization, which was quite novel at the time. He and his business partner employed 185 dentists who worked part-time in their own offices for the DMO, although there was one full-time clinic in Dundalk, MD. I didn't envision my future in mass-production dentistry, but it would pay the bills, especially school loans. This would be a temporary situation until I could establish a quality private practice.

Apparently, I was already hired. He told me in a one-sided conversation that I would work two days a week for him with another day earmarked to start my own practice. Dr. Dolph's trusted assistant of many years, another trophy lass, would assist me. She didn't appreciate it when I showed her the new techniques I'd just learned in school.

"Well. That's not the way we do it *here*," she said in an icy tone.

Despite my advanced degree, I was the bottom rung. Several months later, after sporadic deliberations, Dr. Dolph reluctantly agreed to hire an assistant I could train. I was thrilled.

Meanwhile, I'd gained his confidence as a clinician. He referred difficult cases to me, especially DMO cases that had failed, and with a large pool of dentists, there was no shortage of botched work. But fixing a problem is not as hard as keeping the offended patient happy in the meantime. Dr. Dolph apparently thought I had an aptitude for people-pleasing. But although I was well compensated, it was stressful work, especially when folks spent an inordinate amount of time in the waiting room, which was always packed.

It didn't take long before Dr. Dolph, making buckets of money on his DMO, lost all interest in his private practice. Those patients were subtly thrown my way, lengthening my weekly hours. But that was a good thing—I needed the money. And although I had Mondays off, I frequently received an early-morning phone call.

"Carroll." The receptionist never called me Dr. James. "You're needed here right away. Dr. Dolph (never Rolph) won't be in and the waiting room's already packed."

"You just found this out?"

"He called in sick."

He wasn't sick; he just wasn't interested anymore. And so nearly every Monday, I rushed out the door and arrived late to see patients who were irritated with me. After several weeks, I finally got wise and was showered and dressed by 8:00 a.m., ready for the inevitable call.

By that point, I had a fledgling private practice, the remnants of Rolph's, along with the DMO grind. Starting at only a few hours a week, I now worked six jam-packed days, one of which was a twelve-and-a-half-hour marathon. The half-hour break for dinner on those frenzied Tuesdays seldom materialized, but I was young and motivated (which is code for broke).

I wondered, however, if my new assistant would be able to keep up the pace. But Kate's enthusiasm during her interview proved to be genuine and ongoing, and her undying energy was more than a match for our grueling tempo. A fast learner with a pleasing demeanor, Kate was efficient and immediately liked by patients—a real plus for a young doc. In short, Kate was a blessing.

Still, "Even youths shall faint and be weary, and … utterly fall." I'm not Superman and Kate wasn't Wonder Woman, and we reacted to stressful situations in much the same way, sometimes appropriately and sometimes, well, inappropriately.

When the staff left the office at five o'clock, the two of us worked alone. On one of those interminable DMO Tuesdays, I pulled back the heavy waiting room drapes and saw dark clouds rolling in. The drive home promised to be a bad one and we were running way behind schedule. Through the business window, I caught a glimpse of all the patients still waiting.

"It's gonna be another late night, Kate," I announced.

Just then a middle-aged lady walked through the door with her unruly son in tow. Exhausted, I ducked into Rolph's private office for a quick break.

I had just slumped into his comfy desk chair when Kate came stumbling down the hallway and nearly fell through the door. (At times she could be quite klutzy.) Tears ran freely down her cheeks. Concerned, I bolted upright.

"What happened? You okay?"

She nodded as she cupped her mouth in a futile attempt to muffle laughter. Her entire body convulsed as her free hand grasped the corner of the desk to steady herself. "Go look … check out … the reception window. You've got to see this for yourself." She regained some poise. "But be discreet."

"Right now?"

"Yes, now," she said, dabbing her eyes with Kleenex.

I nonchalantly strolled down the hall and peeked around the corner. The patient's adolescent son had plastered his bulging lips and booger-encrusted nostrils against the windowpane. Flanked by pudgy hands that also pressed on the glass, his bug eyes quivered while a stream of drool trailed slowly down the window. He panted like a basset hound trapped in a car on a hot summer's day.

Caught between this Dalí-like vision and Kate's stifled, yet infectious laughter, I had no hope of maintaining proper decorum before beating a hasty retreat to Rolph's inner sanctuary. Kate followed hard on my heels and we shut the door, looked into each other's eyes, and burst into laughter.

Finally regaining my composure, and without looking straight at her, I affected a serious "doctor" posture and said, "Kate, get the mom back right away. We're getting further backed up."

"Okay," she said, also ready to finish up and go home.

Walking side-by-side, we turned the corner as the boy's lizard-like tongue flicked across the glass. I didn't need to glance at Kate to get her reaction; we made a quick U-turn and staggered back down the hallway, doubling over in fits of mirth.

"I … I'm glad he's not on the schedule," I declared, wiping my eyes. "I'll stay out of sight while you seat her. Whatever you do, don't look directly at the window."

Kate spit laughter through her nose before regaining her composure, brushing back her hair and marching away alone.

I practiced Zen-like breathing before entering the operatory. "Good evening, Ms. Jones. How are you tonight?"

She wasn't offended, or rude, or even nice. In fact, she demonstrated no personality whatsoever. *I wonder if she heard us laughing.*

With reasonable self-control, Kate and I got down to the business at hand. Ms. Jones needed a white filling in her upper front tooth, so I administered a local anesthetic and paused to let it work. An awkward silence ensued; the typical small talk was out of the question. I glanced in every direction except Kate's.

Although I'd developed a certain confidence in her, Kate still required close supervision; she was a quick study, but her training wasn't complete yet. In order for me to see behind the upper front teeth, she had to blow air over my mouth mirror, which otherwise fogs.

"Okay, Kate," I said, "now dry the tooth."

She confidently rotated the angled tip, aimed it upward, and … missed. Compressed air shot up Ms. Jones's nose, billowing out her nostrils. Kate gasped while the lady's eyes bulged like her son's had behind the reception window.

Unable to hold it in, Kate began to rock with laughter. It was a miracle she didn't fall off her stool and onto Ms. Jones. Her infectious reaction made me laugh too, which I tried to disguise as a cough.

"Excuse me, Ms. Jones," I lamely said.

She didn't see the humor and huffed.

After we finished her filling, she made a beeline exit, grabbing her son's hand on the way through the waiting room. She never paused to look back but he did, pressing his chubby face against the glass one last time. His tongue lashed out to the side and quickly drew back, as if he'd caught an insect. More smear ran down the glass before his mother yanked him through the door.

As soon as the door clicked, Kate and I degenerated into hysterics. The patients still waiting must have wondered what was so funny. Maybe they just thought we were a happy team. They would've been right.

The following day, I spent extra time reviewing basic technique with Kate, focusing specifically on the air/water syringe. But the phrase, "Dry the area" still evoked a slight grin and comic relief on particularly tough days.

Yup, Kate worked out just fine.

I even married her.

CHAPTER FIVE

MiL

"Nuthin's stronger than blood."

Clan loyalties can be fierce in southwest Virginia where my mother hails from. For generations, the Arrington's had farmed rocks about forty miles from Tug Valley, the epicenter of the infamous Hatfield and McCoy Feud. But back in Maryland, loyalties were sorely tested when I fished for patients to start my own practice. The family discount didn't get any bites; relatives knew too much about my often mischievous youth. More on that later.

Mischievous. I always thought the term meant harmless fun. But *Webster's 1828 Dictionary* defines it as "harmful; hurtful; injurious." Although I intended no harm with my childhood pranks, they now seemed to matter. My relatives had once seen me and my Michigan cousins blow up an outhouse, for just one example. And after all, we were talking about the dreaded dentist.

"Sooo ... Carroll. How's it goin'? I'd make an appointment, but I've already got a dentist."

"Keeping busy in Dr. Dolph's fancy office?"

"Been sued yet?"

Cousin Clyde was the straight shooter. Having moved to Northern Virginia for a job, Clyde sported a removable partial denture to replace the two front teeth he lost in a bar fight. "But you oughta see the other guy," he always said. When I asked him if he wanted a new partial, he assured me, "It fits just fine, Carroll." But it didn't. In fact, Clyde seldom wore it. He simply didn't want me "fooling 'round in his mouth."

Although he'd been anxious for me to get a job, Dad never came in for an appointment. He figured his dentures would last him a lifetime. Or maybe he didn't trust me any more than my other relations.

Mom, on the other hand, promptly made an appointment for a cleaning. *Maternal pride over sanity?* A tough mountain woman, she didn't seem at all nervous—at least she didn't show it. That prompted a second cousin twice removed, along with a few friends I had badgered, to slowly drift my way. Most, however, kept an ear cocked for any blunders.

"Been to Carroll's office yet?" the first cousin asked.

"No. But my wife's cousin tried him out," the second cousin replied.

"Any screwups?"

"Nope, she's still alive."

"He expensive?"

"He's a dentist."

To her everlasting credit, my mother-in-law, with no blood obligation, scheduled a checkup soon after Kate and I wed. Jean was Arkansas Ozark, close enough to Appalachian, so I felt a certain affinity and was anxious to make a good impression. It's hard to screw up a cleaning; pretty basic stuff. My game plan was to be friendly and caring, all the while maintaining a professional demeanor.

During her initial checkup, I found that Jean was fastidious about brushing and flossing with only a few tiny fillings from years ago—never any major work like root canals, caps, or gum surgery. It wasn't until the end of the visit that she mentioned one minor complaint.

"Carroll ... uh, *Dr.* James," she said with a grin. "I hesitate to even bring it up, but a molar has been aching on and off. It's probably nothing."

Uh oh. I didn't see that coming. "Which one, Jean?"

"Right here, toward the back on the top left," she said, stretching her cheek.

Jean was no complainer, so I knew to take her seriously. I affected a pensive attitude with my pen poised over her chart. "Does it hurt when you chew?"

"Not necessarily."

"Okay, what about hot or cold?"

"No," she said definitively.

"Does it get worse when you lie down?"

"I haven't noticed anything like that."

"Does it ever wake you up during the night or keep you from going to sleep?"

"It's not been that bad."

Ice, heat, and percussion didn't hurt and radiographs at various angles revealed nothing. Finding no obvious reason for her intermittent "discomfort," which is dental-speak for "pain," her chart was now full of scribbles that had become increasingly illegible. *Surely that was impressive.*

Finally, she volunteered, "It sometimes aches for no apparent reason and quickly goes away."

"Ahhh!" I said, as if I'd had an epiphany. A vague, nondescript twinge suggested a simple bruise, which folks could seldom pinpoint. However, Jean consistently pointed to the same tooth. I probed deeper.

"You're digging into my gums, Carroll!"

So much for "Dr. James."

It wasn't going to be an easy diagnosis, but I had to say something definitive. After all, I was the sharp young doctor trained in the latest techniques. "Maybe additional symptoms will come to light if we give it more time," I said. Time, of course, was the quintessential medical cop-out.

She stared at me as if to say, *This is the best you can come up with?*

I was confident that there was no infection and didn't want to rush into any treatment that might have been unnecessary, so I said, "Promise me you'll report back right away if new symptoms develop. It's vital to know exactly when or if it takes a turn for the worse."

Lame.

She agreed and, if nothing else, appeared satisfied with my non-advice advice. "Thank you," she said with a smile as she got up to leave.

But I wasn't satisfied. The easy "everything is fine, see ya in six months" checkup I'd hoped for had failed to materialize. Then again, maybe I was right and it was a simple bruise; I'd look the hero when it went away.

Fat chance! St. Apollonia, the Patron Saint of dentists, wasn't going to let me off that easy.

On a crisp autumn afternoon, Kate and I drove to my in-laws' home for Sunday supper. The sun's warm rays filtered through the shimmering red and gold of the maple trees, lending a pastoral air to the Lord's Day. Jean's cheerful greeting glowed, mirroring the stand of burning bushes behind their brick home. "Come on in. Frank's in the sunroom watching football, Carroll."

"Thanks. Something sure smells good." I smiled and headed for the enclosed porch around back and plopped down on the couch as the second half of the Redskins game began. I asked Frank, Kate's dad, "So, who's winning?"

"The Skins. Who else?"

Stupid question. Joe Gibbs was coaching, so of course they were winning.

Frank grabbed a handful of beer nuts and chased them with a pull on his scotch on the rocks. Kate's mom promptly showed up with a beer for me, the perfect complement to the chips and salsa she placed on the coffee table. Dinner would have to wait until the game was over.

It was worth the wait. The Skins won. After we devoured the meal, Jean, ever the gracious host, subtly got up to clear the table. "Everyone just stay put while I tidy up a bit. I'll fetch dessert shortly," she said.

Although Frank was antsy for his wife's warm homemade pumpkin pie à la mode, she served me first. I dug in and had just stuffed my face when she paused by my chair, balancing several dirty serving plates in her hands.

"You know, Carroll," she said unobtrusively, "that tooth is still the same."

I tensed as a large chunk of pie—humble pie—squeezed down my throat and landed with a thud. I put my fork down and looked up. "That's a shame, Jean. Call the office tomorrow morning and we'll take another look." I stared down as my ice cream melted over the hot piecrust.

Frank quickly polished his off and said, "You going to finish yours, Carroll?"

"Nah. I'm stuffed," I replied, shoving my plate toward him. His slight frame belied a healthy appetite; the man could eat anything and not gain a pound.

Jean popped into the office later that week. *Something must've changed for her to bring it up at supper*, I mused. *This could be a good thing.*

But I probed and prodded and found nothing. A follow-up radiograph proved worthless. Her answers were verbatim to my progress notes, but I couldn't simply do nothing.

"Jean, has the pain gotten more intense?"

"Not really," she quietly said.

So why'd you bring it up over dessert? I thought. "Let's give it a little more time," I said, trying to sound sincere.

Although she knew my response was a cop-out, her smile was a beacon of graciousness, which made me feel that much worse.

She returned a couple months later for her regular six-month checkup. She had the same impeccable home care, with no cavities or gum disease.

"Everything's fine, Carroll," Jean said. "Well ... that one little thing still bothers that same tooth."

Oh God, no!

That wayward tooth had continued to act up without getting any better or worse. "Time" hadn't done the trick. Another radiograph (*Is this three or four?*) yielded absolutely nothing. I almost hoped to see an abscess, which could at least be treated. As I had been in practice for only a short time, I knew I probably looked naïve or incompetent; I certainly felt I was and feared I wasn't making any points with my young bride.

I guess it's called practice because you never quite get it right, I thought, wondering what I had overlooked.

Then I came out with, "Let's try an oral rinse and nutritional supplements, along with a regimen of broad-spectrum antibiotics for that low-grade sinus infection."

What sinus infection?

But without questioning the wisdom of my shotgun approach, Jean cheerfully agreed. I reasoned that if it was psychological, a placebo just might do the trick. Only time would tell, though that tack hadn't worked out so well.

That afternoon, Kate asked, "What do you think about Mom's tooth?"

I reluctantly related several diagnostic possibilities along with my proposed non-treatment treatment.

"Honestly, I don't know if it'll work." I felt defensive. "Look, Kate. It might've been an actual pain at first. But it's probably all in her head now."

Husbands can be so dumb.

Kate shot me a piqued look, but I continued to dig a hole.

"A lot of things are psychosomatic, you know."

Kate's whole body tensed as her eyes narrowed. Thinking that my medico-technical jargon had impressed her, I completely misread her.

"Even if it was a hyperemia—that's a bruise, Kate," I said condescendingly, not yet having learned that Latin doesn't actually make a doctor look good, "it has evolved into a ghost pain that's stored in the cerebral cortex as leftover baggage."

I was sort of happy with the way I'd handled it.

Kate, on the other hand, was way beyond insult. She firmly planted her hands on her curvy hips and leaned toward me, somehow appearing taller. "Are you suggesting that my mother is a basket case?"

"Uh, no. I just thought ..."

"Do you honestly think all women are ditzy?"

A collision was in the making. It was time to backpedal.

"Well, no. This might ... uh, does happen with men as well," I said. But instead of leaving it there, I continued, "But I don't think it happens as often with men."

What the hell was I thinking?

Mark Twain once said, "It's better to keep your mouth shut and appear stupid than open it and remove all doubt." Good advice.

My agitated spouse then spewed a series of abusive epithets, none of which I can remember. And if I could, I couldn't repeat them. I looked for cover, but saw nowhere to go. My honest defense had been tried and found wanting. Tired and frustrated, I blurted, "Your mother is simply neurotic! There's no other explanation."

If you've never experienced the icy silence of a wife scorned, try dissing her beloved mom. It was too late when it dawned on me that I'd committed a serious breach of mother-in-law etiquette. I felt blood drain from my face as Kate stormed off. Her cold shoulder continued throughout the afternoon, and she spoke not a word to me during the long ride home.

After a lonely dinner of PB&J, I went out back and read until late, then crept into bed once Kate was asleep. It took several days for things to thaw.

Several months elapsed and I'd almost forgotten the whole thing when I saw Jean's name posted on the day schedule: TA–toothache. Kate had also highlighted it with a red Sharpie.

Oh no! A cloud of gloom slowly enveloped me as the day dragged on. When it was her appointed time, I ducked into my private office to call an oral surgeon with an answer to a question. It was a delaying tactic; I could've called him back anytime.

Kate seated her mom while I cowered in my office and thought about hitting the head. *Can't put this off forever, Carroll.* Slump-shouldered, I shuffled into the operatory wishing I was anywhere but there.

"Good afternoon, Jean," I said sheepishly.

She tilted her head toward me and with the sweetest countenance ever seen, pointing to her left cheek. I bent over, adjusted the mouth light, and saw that the inner wall of her upper first molar—our old friend—was gone. My mouth dropped as Jean retrieved a folded tissue from her purse. "I was wondering if you needed this?" she asked. Carefully preserved in the napkin was the jagged piece of tooth that had sheared off.

"No," I said.

A microscopic fracture had caused her pain from the get-go. I babbled an explanation.

"A hairline fracture is impossible to detect clinically, even with radiographs. No way to know until it actually breaks ..."

She continued to smile throughout my prattle.

"Let's smooth it off for now," I offered. After I filed it down, an uncomfortable silence ensued, which I decided to fill with more inane rambling. "Happens all the time you know. Teeth chip for no apparent reason."

Kate stood in the background, shaking her head. I had to do something to assure them both that I knew what I was doing.

"After it's properly restored with a crown, the sensitivity will abate and you'll be able to eat normally," I said hopefully.

When I finally stopped to take a deep breath, Jean proclaimed, with a twinkle in her eyes, "You see. I am not *neurotic*!"

Blood drained from my face as I realized that Kate had told her what I'd said in frustration. Weak-kneed, I plopped onto my stool as it dawned on me that Kate told her mother *everything*.

From that day forth I have never, ever—even jokingly—referred to any patient as neurotic … especially not kinfolk.

CHAPTER SIX

The Handwriting on the Wall

When I gave Dr. Dolph my three months' notice, he was so angry that he fired me from the DMO, giving me a week to leave whether I had finished work already started on my patients or not. Suddenly finding my fledgling practice homeless, I frantically searched for office space. All I found was a new, unfinished medical building, the owners of which asked a heap of money to build my suite. Not only that, it would take months to complete.

Having no choice, I ran up debts to the landlord, architect, banker, accountant, lawyer, plumbers, electricians, carpenters, etc.; the federal, state, county, and city fees were exorbitant, in addition to the large deposits I had to give utility companies. Equipment, instruments, and professional supplies were the final budget busters. Second-hand furniture would have to make do.

Chronically late construction workers, sometimes shoddy work, and never-ending hassles with inspectors seemed to go on forever, but the place slowly came together. Then, a few disgruntled neighbors cast a pall over the whole endeavor.

Early one morning I arrived at Minor Medical Building to an eerie stillness; there was no construction noise, not even a hammer pounding. I found a red-lettered notice posted on the door of my almost-completed, first floor office.

"All construction is prohibited until further notice."

Kate and I had already scheduled a few patients in anticipation of opening, but now they would have to be postponed—indefinitely. Hope faded.

The surrounding residents had complained about a commercial facility and noticed that the handicap access didn't satisfy newly updated codes. The landlord applied for an exception, but that takes time. Our small patient base dissipated into the ether—not that I could blame them.

Miraculously, the stop order was soon lifted and my dental chair was installed. Things were looking up as my brother, Lee, and I unloaded used waiting room furniture from his pickup.

With my office in place, and eager to deliver high-quality treatment, I still lacked one thing: patients. Surprisingly, a few loyal folks had hung in there but not enough to pay the bills, not to mention those staggering school loans that would take fifteen years to pay off.

As cruel icing on the cake, the high-tech telephones with their multiline/multifunction setup I'd spent so much on, foisted on me by a slick salesman, didn't seem to work. (In my frustration, I envisioned stringing a phone cord around his scrawny neck, then thought better of it.) To test them out, I called Kate, who was at the office waiting for a patient—any patient—to call. When she put me on hold because the other line rang, I became excited.

"Sorry, Carroll," Kate said. "That was Dominoes with a two-for-one deal on delivery of large lunch pizzas."

I couldn't even afford that.

I tried a couple of publicity stunts that went nowhere, and advertising was considered beneath a doctor's dignity in the 1970s, so although I remained adamantly opposed to DMOs, especially after the unethical practices I had seen with my former boss—"just clean the front ones because that's all they care about," he'd said—something had to be done or I would go bankrupt.

For short stretches I was busy enough to keep my head above water. Then the phones would again go on strike. Casework was lucrative but scarce; what I needed was a consistent patient flow. As the roller-coaster ride continued, melancholy gave way to depression and I began pacing like I had when I was waiting for my license.

The trade journals were full of articles by gurus who promised, "Ten Easy Steps to Attract Twelve New Patients a Week." Never happened, but I did manage to spend a lot of the bank's money on various subscriptions.

Although Kate remained upbeat—a Pollyanna to my Eeyore—my mood didn't improve when classmates bragged about their booming practices. I consoled myself with the knowledge that they'd joined numerous dental plans—of course they were buying homes, taking exotic vacations, and eating real food while I stalked in circles and lost weight. But "All good things come to those who wait," right?

I must've been anticipating some pretty good things.

During the slow periods—most of the time—I retreated to my private office to brood in solitude. With a heavy heart, I'd plop my butt down on the soft leather chair behind my oak desk. They were the only furnishings I hadn't skimped on.

I wrestled with confused emotions. *What was I thinking when I went into dentistry?* But then I'd remember the pride on Grandma's face, the new patients who were always an emotional lift—chatting about spouses, children, pets, and homes always pulled me out of the doldrums. But I quickly regressed when I had too much time to fret.

One day while I sat slouched behind my desk, Kate disturbed my sulking by barging in. She hadn't even knocked before sailing past the distinctly marked Private sign.

"Isn't it obvious I don't want to be disturbed?" I said.

She tried to lift the pervasive gloom by announcing the latest news from the front desk with a smile. "The afternoon patient just canceled. You can take a break."

A break! I steamed without saying it. *A break from what?* The whole day—the whole week—had been free time. And this wasn't just any cancelation; it was an extensive case that I'd counted on to pay a few overdue bills. In no frame of mind to be cheered up, I growled, "Leave me be."

Proudly displayed on my desktop was an elegant pen duo—ballpoint and fountain—mounted in a classic marble base. Kate's aunt had presented it to me at our grand opening, a celebration that now seemed premature.

Despite looking sophisticated on my desk, the archaic device that sucks ink into the fountain pen from an inkwell was seldom used anymore. Only a skilled calligrapher could properly wield it without trailing ink all over the paper. With too much time on my hands, I had repeatedly pumped the lever, loading it to the max.

Determined to keep me from sinking further into despair, Kate displayed an exaggerated frown as she snatched the fountain pen to make her point. "You need to lighten up, Carroll," she said teasingly, crisply flicking the pen for emphasis.

A jet-black stream shot from the pen's slotted tip, not only streaking my face, neck, and glasses, but leaving a black line down my shirt and a speckled trail across my brand-new highly polished desk.

I sat stunned while a smudge drifted slowly down one lens, distorting Kate's figure, as if I were looking at her through a glass darkly. She gasped, and with my unobstructed eye, I noticed a look of horror contorting her pretty face.

In a clumsy attempt to recover, she snapped her wrist in reverse, whipping the pen upward to deliver a second line across the desk, my body, and the other lens. The momentum continued skyward to trace an ever-widening stripe of black goo up the freshly painted wall and onto the ceiling.

Through the two oozing blobs of India ink, I could barely see Kate covering her mouth. Knowing it was an accident, I tried to remain calm and slowly removed my glasses. Then I saw that instead of being horrified, she was actually covering her mouth to stifle a laugh. "I think I'm going to wet my pants!" she managed to sputter.

No longer able to contain herself, she bolted for the restroom, holding her sides. "I'm so sorry!" she squealed.

But I don't think she was. She knew I needed a good laugh in the worst way ... and the worst way was how I got it.

Kate's reaction was infectious and the humor of it slowly dawned on me. Although I tried not to crack a smile, her shenanigans were like a refreshing breeze in the midst of summer blues.

When she returned from the ladies room, she bore a handful of tissues to clean my face, which only further smeared the goop. I wiped my own glasses and grinned sheepishly, but I still couldn't bring myself to laugh out loud.

In the midst of unproductive worry, Kate had unwittingly gotten me back on my feet, and I had received a lesson in the splattered ink: There's more to a person's overall well-being than "stuff" or perceived success—love, joy, and laughter count for much more.

Business eventually picked up, and it not only became successful, but personally satisfying too. That broad band of ink on the ceiling has faded, but it's still there. Whenever life's pressures start to get me down, all I have to do is lean back and look up. A slight grin will creep across my face, and sometimes I chuckle softly.

I've not, however, ever refilled the fountain pen.

CHAPTER SEVEN

Dr. Frieden

My buddy Stan couldn't believe his horned-rimmed eyes. His new fifty-pound X-ray head had drifted down onto his patient's lap and pinned him to the dental chair. Stan pulled while his elderly patient frantically pushed. With the help of his petite assistant, the three of them wrestled it to the floor.

Although Stan's equipment was state of the art, his construction had been done on the cheap. He'd hired a friend who was an unlicensed contractor to convert the neglected half of an ancient ranch house into a dental office; the other half housed an Italian restaurant whose kitchen divided the two halves. The result? Patients could have dental work, along with pasta and a glass of merlot.

Although his erstwhile handyman had announced that the walls were "good 'n' strong—jus' need a little dressing up is all," when Stan's assistant extended the heavy X-ray head to shoot a film, the resulting strain was too much on the walls, which ballooned like an aneurysm and clouded the operatory with crumbling plaster dust.

Thankfully, Stan's patient was a friend who had a good

sense of humor. He gave him a discount and didn't charge anything for the radiographs, which he took at a later date.

A few years later, Stan's practice had grown exponentially, forcing him to move to a new location. This time, he hired a bonded carpenter who grandly proclaimed, "I got this place built like a fort. Them studs is equal to the task." But on Stan's second opening day, he once again found an unwitting patient firmly pinned to the dental chair by the X-ray. Even late-night wrestling isn't this predictable. The victim? The same old guy as before. Stan gave him another discount.

Determined not to repeat Stan's structural mishaps, I instructed my carpenter to beef up the walls with double two by eights when I located to an upscale suburb. He argued with me, saying, "That's overkill. You trying to shore up the Bay Bridge?"

"Yes," I insisted.

I've had no crushed patients to date.

As Minor Medical Building neared completion, the landlord radically raised the rent on the few remaining suites still unleased. Dr. Frieden, also a dentist, got the last one, which was across the hall from mine. The construction noise, which had only recently been music to my ears, would soon pass.

Dr. Frieden, well into his fifties, had always worked for the government or one of those storefront chains that were popping up like weeds. Now, however, he decided to try his hand at private practice. It would have been fine, except that time wasn't on his side. The truth is, it takes youthful energy to launch the backbreaking business of dentistry; Dr. Frieden's endeavor would not only be exhausting, but it would be at the expense of second and third mortgages on his home. But his dream was not to be denied.

Not long after, the noise ceased and he proudly hung a

shingle on his door: *Dr. Frieden, DDS*. When I moseyed over to meet and congratulate him, I found his office locked but later ran into him in the parking lot.

"Hi, I'm Carroll James," I said, offering my hand.

"Glad to meet you," he said with a smile. "I'm waiting for an occupancy permit." *I know that song*, I thought. "Should be open in a day or so." *You hope.*

Then I added with encouragement, "Looking forward to seeing your suite."

Soon after his permit was issued, however, I didn't see any folks coming and going from his office. *His patient base must be even smaller than mine*, I thought.

Shaded by ancient oak trees, Minor Medical was in a residential neighborhood, and my office windows looked out on the tenant parking lot immediately out back. The asphalt wasn't picturesque, but the view of homes was better than Dr. Rolph's non-view had been; the only window in Dolph's place was in the waiting room and I seldom went in there. Gazing outdoors is a nice break from dentistry's cramped venue. Yawning mouths and sterile walls can be a bit claustrophobic.

On one bright, cheery day while my patient was rinsing into the cuspidor, I glanced out at the squirrels scampering along the privacy fence and saw portly Dr. Frieden standing motionless in the parking lot, his silhouette reminiscent of Alfred Hitchcock. Catatonically focused on the trunk of his old beat-up car (the fenders and door panels were of different colors with primer gray as the prevalent mood), he suddenly became animated and slammed his fist on the trunk. The tired hinges groaned as the battered lid struggled to open. He stared into the depths of the trunk for what seemed an eternity, then reached in and retrieved a weather-beaten golf bag.

I mechanically holstered my drill and leaned back to watch as the open-air drama developed. My patient had finished rinsing and asked, "What's up?"

"Dunno. Check out the parking lot and see if you can figure it out."

Dr. Frieden dug out an old golf ball that sported a number of smiley faces carved by a club. He placed it directly on the hard pavement, threatening a practice shot that invited total destruction to the club. (The old clubs might've fetched a pretty penny from an antique dealer if they'd been in decent shape; they weren't.)

Anticipating a *coup de grace* for the aging equipment, my patient, an accomplished golfer, leaned forward to watch. He, Kate, and I tensed as the doc twisted slowly into a perfect backswing. Reversing, he swung in slo-mo and performed an unblemished follow-through without hitting the pavement.

He then took a half step forward and formally addressed the ball.

"Uh oh. He's actually gonna hit it this time," I muttered. But instead of swinging, he stood stock-still, like Lot's wife when she turned to look at Sodom and Gomorrah and turned into a pillar of salt. After this interlude, he gently tapped the ball and it slowly rolled under the car. He then placed a protective sock over the club head (it might've been a real sock) and gingerly placed the cracked leather bag back into the trunk.

On certain days, he repeated this cheerful diversion to the delight of my patients, the staff, and me.

A few weeks later, I went across the hall to visit and discovered that Dr. Frieden's waiting room, in complement to his golf clubs, was decorated in early flea market. A couple of old wooden chairs sat on a floor covered with myriad loose carpet samples of no standard size, allowing the underlying concrete to show through the gaps. The motley assortment of colors, designs, textures, and patterns—blue, green, red, yellow, mauve, checked, striped, spotted, and plain—lent a chaotic, Wonderland-like aura.

I searched the room for a reception window and discovered only a simple door disguised by the same monochrome paint as the walls: autumn wheat. After tripping on an exposed edge of the Byzantine floor, and to avoid any more pitfalls, I stepped high like a Lipizzaner. There should've been a sign on the hall door: ENTER AT YOUR OWN RISK.

I knocked on the inside door, softly at first. No response. I rapped a little louder. Still nothing. My imagination took flight, half expecting a large white rabbit to pop through a gap in the animated floor. *Guess he's not in.*

But as I turned to leave, the door suddenly flew open. Standing in the entranceway, sporting a broad smile, was a balding, five-foot-ten rabbit in a white tunic.

It took me a moment to realize it was Dr. Frieden.

With a firm handshake and hefty slap on the back, he said, "Come on in, Carroll. Glad you could stop by. I've seen you through those nice big windows. You're pretty busy over there."

I hoped he hadn't noticed us staring at him. "Just wanted to say hi," I managed.

"Wanna take a tour?" He was obviously delighted with his accomplishment.

"Sure. I'd love to."

The tricky terrain continued. When I again tripped on a remnant, he caught my arm, smiled, and said, "Watch your step, Carroll."

His only treatment room was straight back, across a narrow hallway. I looked in and thought, *Is this a family room or an operatory?*

An old console TV, shoved against the near wall, had been conscripted as a countertop with far too many instruments piled on the faux-wood top. I eyeballed the large on-off knob to the right of the semi-round screen and considered pulling it just to see if the TV worked. Upon more sober reflection, though, I decided not to; the sonorous *click* might've sent instruments tumbling to the floor. As it was, the room smelled musty and I had to squeeze my nose to forestall a sneeze.

The dental chair was operated by a pump-action foot pedal and resembled an old barber's chair, except it had those little black round things with which to trap a patient's head. The seat cushion had an adhesive fabric strip on it. *At least it isn't duct tape.*

The porcelain cuspidor was the size of a birdbath and resembled a spittoon. What's more, the bulky, freestanding X-ray machine looked as if it would emit Dr. Frankenstein-like crackling sounds. If it were to fall, like Stan's had, it would surely kill. The archaic belt-driven drill promised to vibrate a patient half to death.

Reminiscent of the 1950s, it was all too recent to be antebellum, but not old enough to be quaint. And to top it all off, there was no sink. The only place to wash hands or instruments was down the hall in the lavatory, where the washbasin was ringed with instruments while another pile sat on the back of the commode. I wondered how a modern professional could practice in such a disorganized, bacteria-friendly venue. Then again, he didn't work all that often. It's safe to say he didn't have an equipment mortgage.

"Thanks for showing me around, Doc," I said. "It's real ... nice. I'd better get back to the office for a patient due about now." *Okay, so it was a white lie.*

"You've got a patient waiting—good for you. Stop in anytime."

I carefully negotiated the moonscape on the way out.

As the Christmas and New Year holidays were approaching, a particularly gloomy, rainy day rolled around. My schedule was lighter than usual, and it had been a while since I'd last called on the old golfer. Now that the cold weather had set in, I hadn't seen him in the parking lot lately either.

Cheerful despite the gloom, I walked into Doc Frieden's waiting room (being prone to motion sickness, I avoided looking down at the vertigo-inducing carpet). His interior door was slightly ajar, so I pulled it open a bit more and softly called, "Doc, you back here?"

There was no answer, so I spoke a little louder. "Hello. Anybody home?"

It was quiet—too quiet; not a soul was in the operatory/ family room. To the right, the storage closet was closed, but to the left the bathroom door stood wide open. I saw a pair of bony knees with polka dot boxers draped around the ankles. Dr. Frieden sat calmly on his porcelain throne, absorbed in a golfing magazine propped on his lap. He was so oblivious to my presence that anyone could've ventured in.

I quietly backed away, fled across the hallway, and stumbled through my lab door laughing. Kate came running.

"You okay?"

With tears streaming down my face, I tried to describe the scene to which I'd just been privy. "He's just sitting there … humming … polka dots …"

Kate's folded arms and sideways look implied that I must be exaggerating.

"Go see for yourself," I said.

"I'll pass," she said, realizing I couldn't have made up something that absurd.

Arriving for work on a crisp winter morning a couple months later, I squeezed my car past a moving van parked out front. Two burly, tattooed men struggled to lift an out-of-date dental chair over multiple carpet samples scattered on the truck floor. Standing beside the truck with his eyes downcast and shoulders slumped, Dr. Frieden mumbled, "I think I'm gonna retire."

Although I was sad to see him go—he was a nice guy, after all—he made the right decision. I shook his hand. "I hope the best for you and that you enjoy your retirement."

He responded with a half-smile.

I imagined him playing a lot of golf, but I admit I wouldn't have wanted to be stuck behind him on the links while he stared interminably at an old ball perched atop a splintered tee. I do miss watching him in the parking lot, though.

CHAPTER EIGHT

Headphones

Kate seated Lori, a stylish young woman who looked unusually haggard that day.

"I didn't sleep a wink last night just thinking about this root canal," she confided.

Kate empathized and handed her a Walkman with padded Boise headphones. "You can listen to music instead of the drill," Kate said with a comforting smile.

Lori nervously sighed. "You guys are so nice. Maybe this won't be so bad."

In the early 1900s, "white noise" was introduced as a distraction to put patients at ease. But the irritating hiss was really no more relaxing than the grinding of a dental drill. The invention of portable tape players, however, offered a choice of real music, and patients could crank the volume ever higher in tandem with the drill's high-pitched whine. As a result, we would have to lift one ear pad to give instructions to "open wide" or "rinse." What's more, some folks—especially teens and young adults—would start foot tapping, which was a drawback because it's hard to perform delicate work on a moving target.

"We'll do our best to make you comfortable," Kate said,

softly placing her hand on Lori's shoulder. "If you need a break, just raise your left hand and I'll have the doctor stop."

"Thanks," Lori said with a crooked smile as the Novocain began to take effect.

While the anesthetic performed its magic, Kate arranged instruments and laid several alcohol-gauze pads on the counter.

"You should be good and numb by now, Lori," I said. "We'll go ahead and get started."

"Okay," she said nervously. Her hands trembled as she positioned the headphones and leaned back. The preparation of the tooth was uneventful and soon finished. While I irrigated the canal with a mild disinfectant, Kate lifted Lori's left ear pad. "Relax, Lori. The worst is over. No more drill." Those once apprehensive eyes softly closed as her body relaxed and Lynyrd Skynyrd's "Sweet Home Alabama" blared from her headset.

It was time to seal the canals with gutta-percha, a gum-like resin. At that time, dentists heated a condenser over an open flame to soften it, creating a tight seal in the canals, but safely maneuvering a red-hot branding iron into someone's mouth can be a little dicey. Steady hands are the keys to success.

As open flames are not a dentist's best friend, we always lit the Bunsen burner at the last moment. Kate struck the match, which sparked, fizzled, then went out. Afraid to press hard on the sulfurous tip, she reluctantly struck again, and another puff of unproductive smoke floated up. A little perturbed, I glanced back to see what the delay was. Kate looked a bit embarrassed and struck the third match with renewed determination—and success. Firing up the propane, she gave me a triumphant look that implied, *See, I did it.* Ever cautious, she placed the burning match on a piece of wet gauze to put it out—wet with alcohol, that is. In an instant, her victory grin turned south as the gauze burst into flame.

Kate jumped from her chair, her elbow knocking into the blazing burner. It thankfully remained upright, keeping the fire confined to a small piece of cloth on the Formica. "Grab it and throw it into the sink," I said quietly through gritted teeth. As a kid, I'd played with fire so much that it didn't seem unusual, but Kate thought otherwise, never having grabbed a fiery brand with her bare hands before. Frozen in place, she stared at the flame while Lori's eyes remained closed in detached reverie, completely unaware.

"*Lord, I'm comin' home to you* ..."

"In the sink," I urged in a whisper. "Do it now!"

Kate snatched the flaming gauze and aimed for the steel sink, but it fell short and landed on a dry paper towel. The liquid spread like ... well, like wildfire.

Somehow overcoming her fear, Kate grasped the non-burning end of the towel and gave a mighty heave. The torch traced a fiery arc over the sink and landed on the other side of it, hard by the wall. During its short flight, the breeze further fanned the flames.

Who knew that wallpaper would burn so readily?

As the conflagration licked up the operatory wall, I envisioned my new office ignominiously vanishing into the shrouds of hell. I jumped out of my chair and pitched the bonfire into the sink. Then I quickly filled a green mixing bowl and splashed water on the wall, a handy lesson I'd learned when Oleander Jacob's hair caught on fire.

With disaster narrowly averted, I glanced at Kate and managed a weak smile, too relieved to be angry. We breathed a collective sigh as I sat back on my stool—until we noticed Lori sniffing like a bloodhound. Her eyes fluttered open while she pulled one of the earpieces away. "Is something burning?"

"No, Lori," I said, affecting a calmness I didn't feel. "Everything's just fine. We're simply getting ready for the final phase."

Lame. But the best I could muster.

Satisfied, she went back to her music and drifted off while we finished the root canal without further incident.

Upon leaving, she commented on how much she enjoyed using the tape player. "You and Kate make a great team, Dr. James."

Sure—a team of firefighters.

"Thanks so much," I said. "And you're a terrific patient."

Like the ink on the ceiling of my office, that burnt smudge on the wallpaper is still there.

CHAPTER NINE

The Move

Kate and I purchased our first home in Pyleton, a small bedroom community surrounded by farmland about an hour from DC. A few miles upstream was the only ferry that remained working on the Potomac watershed—the battle-gray flatboat, powered by a diesel engine in a rowboat attached to the side, carried fifteen average-sized cars.

Right after we moved, two enormous gravel trucks approached from the Virginia side. The captain scratched his beer belly and spit tobacco juice. "Load 'em both," he said.

Bad idea.

The *Stonewall*—the ferry was owned and operated by an admirer of the general—chugged away from the ramp and promptly slid straight under the water. Waves gently lapped against the boat's protruding rails while both trucks' tires seemingly walked on water.

The disaster featured prominently on the front page of the *Pyleton News*, our four-page tabloid, where a grainy black and white photo showed a crane unloading the waterlogged trucks. It took a couple of days, but the *Stonewall* finally floated to the surface and was back in business—with a new helmsman.

Water-related stories seemed to be the most prevalent in our sleepy town; in fact, water consumption stole most headlines in the *News* during the dry summer months. If one of the five public wells fell below a critical level, the paper would announce, "Anyone caught watering their lawn will be fined $50," with the fine-print concession: "Payable in two easy installments."

Another article warned, "Anyone washing a car must replenish the water." I had to wonder, *How ya gonna do that?* But one good ole boy, tired of farming, thought he could make a go of a car wash and built a self-service variety on Main Street. Forced to remain idle for half the summer, though, it soon failed, and the ugly block structure stood empty for years as a reminder to residents to keep their garden hoses stowed during the dry months.

The *News* also featured myriad community organizations and their activities: Boy Scouts, Girl Scouts, Odd Fellows, Lions Club, church bazaars, and the vaunted Pyleton Piranha Swim Team (I always wondered if there was a special concession for water for the pool).

In Floyd's Barbershop, an old red-brick building at the four-way stop, customers could catch up on *Field & Stream*, *Guns & Gardens*, and rumors. (Floyd quickly removed any *People* magazines left behind—too unseemly.)

Did I mention it was a small town?

Above the barbershop, an Odd Fellows Hall was located next to the second-floor dental office; both shared a street-level door that opened to a narrow staircase. The smell of hair tonics, kitchen grease, and dental clove wafted along Main Street. Dr. Patel, the dentist, practiced only two days a week, so I sublet his office and equipment on Thursdays, while a podiatrist, Dr. Heel (no kidding), leased space on Wednesdays.

Right after Kate and I wed, Dr. Patel blindsided me by packing up and leaving town with only two weeks' notice. This left Kate to notify my patients that they'd now have to drive twenty miles to my Rockville office. We entertained the idea of having a home office, but our current house wasn't large enough. So while Kate searched for a bigger house to accommodate the idea, most of my patients found a dentist closer than Rockville.

So much for starting with a bang.

As we prepared to move after barely arriving, Jim, our neighbor from Brooklyn three doors down, took it personally. "What's wrong wit' us?" he asked.

"Nuthin'," I said. "It's just that I can't put a dental office in a townhouse—"

"You'se make me sick," he said with a sneer. "I taught we was friends."

Tough crowd.

After our realtor staked a For Sale sign in our front lawn, it disappeared. He staked another. It disappeared. Finally, he put a sign inside the window.

Was it Jim? Was he that torn up over our leaving?

Probably not. Plus he was cop. But since the culprit was never discovered, I always kind of wondered.

After all, Jim was quite a character ...

A diehard Giants fan who loathed the Redskins at a time when Joe Gibb's team was winning big, Jim gloated when Joe Theisman's leg was accidentally snapped by the Giants' Lawrence Taylor (who was truly remorseful). In fact, he kept a videotape of the scene to bring out at parties.

Not only did Jim sometimes find humor in others' misfortune, he also poked fun at my subtle southern accent, the way my "Joisey" friends had. He automatically accused anyone with a "hick accent" of bigotry, which was ironic because he patrolled DC's inner city with a big German Shepherd he named Sambo, who was actually quite cuddly—Sambo, not Jim.

"Sooo ... Jim," I asked him once, "how do you get Sambo into working mode?"

With an evil smirk he spelled, "A-t-t-a-c-k."

Not surprisingly, Jim and Wanda's townhouse was never vandalized.

They liked to party hearty, filling their house with rowdy revelers. George, who had a great sense of humor, had sold us our house. He and his wife Ann, who were our bowling partners, were compassionate folks who were active in their diocese and local charities.

At one party, George and I were chatting about my furnace problems when George tipped his Solo cup, found it empty, and headed toward the keg. "You want another one, Carroll?"

"Nah. I'm fine. Maybe later."

After awhile, I thought again of my heating issues and asked of no one in particular, "I wonder where George went off to?"

Jim's wife leaned into me. "Oh, heesh schlepped ou' back ta water the bushes."

She'd had a few by then.

More time passed and Ann found me standing alone in a corner. "Have you seen my adolescent husband, Carroll?" She looked a bit concerned. George had imbibed more than usual that night.

"I'll look around," I said. "I heard he might be out back."

"Thanks. He's probably okay, but just to be sure ..."

Jim's postage-stamp-sized backyard bordered the high school athletic fields, and without the game lights on, it was quite dark. Stepping into the black of a crisp, cool evening, I saw that Sambo's cage was open. *That's odd*, I thought. Then I noticed two legs splayed across the grass. Sambo was straddling them, his front paws firmly planted on his victim's chest. His tail wasn't wagging and his face hung only inches from George's.

Fairly inebriated, George had stumbled against the unlatched gate and landed halfway inside the cage. Sambo probably had George trapped like this since he staggered into his pen out back. His distinct, gravelly voice punctuated the darkness. "Help me. Please, for God's sake, help."

Sambo growled. He never acknowledged my presence and I didn't try to coax him off. The only command I was aware he knew—"A-t-t-a-c-k"—wouldn't help George much.

"I'll get Jim straightaway. Now don't you go anywhere," I said to George as I ran inside. I looked over the heads of the dense throng of revelers and saw Jim on the far side of the living room, hanging onto the couch and swaying.

"Hey, Jim! Sambo's got George trapped out back."

"Wha'? Can't hear you'se."

"Sambo's pinned George to the ground," I yelled. "Get out there."

As Jim teetered into the backyard, a big grin spread across his flushed face. "What'll ya give me ta get him off, George?"

"That's not funny, you dumb son of a bitch." George was in no mood to negotiate.

Sambo growled louder.

"I'd keep your voice down, Georgie boy," Jim said. "Sambo don't like yellin'."

George softly pleaded, "I'll buy ya a beer or two. Just git him off me."

"Fair enough. But I'll be 'specting those beers." Jim got serious. "Sambo! Release!" The shepherd instantly sat down and nuzzled Jim's hand.

Well, that was easy.

I felt stupid as George stood up, zipped up, and then more or less walked inside to find Ann. "Let's go home," he said.

After a few months, Kate found an affordable house just outside town. Jim gave us more grief. "Movin' to the fancy neighborhood?"

"It's only four blocks away, Jim," I said, "and it's not fancy."

"Whatever," he said with a grumble.

Since our contract to buy the new house was contingent on

selling our current one—and we only had ninety days to do it—we were distressed when nearly three months passed without a nibble on our place. I suspected Jim might've chased off a prospective buyer or two—he and Sambo were hanging out in the front yard more than usual.

"Ya know, Carroll," Jim said one day, putting his foot on our second For Sale sign, "a storm blew down our row of houses before they were finished. Hard to sell a place been knocked over by a little wind."

I stared up at the town's looming water tower. As a strong gust kicked up, I thought that maybe I should lower the asking price.

But just before our contract expired, fate interceded. A teenager sped into town, missed the tight turn, and clobbered the old house we were supposed to move into, which now had to have major repairs. Before that work was completed, a tractor trailer jackknifed into it. It was clearly never meant to be ours, so we let the contract lapse and Kate continued to scan the real estate listings.

After returning home from church on a fine Sunday afternoon, we plopped down on the couch, secretly hoping the other would slap a couple of sandwiches together.

"You hungry?"

"Nah."

"Yeah, me neither," she smiled while shaking out the Sunday paper. She soon found an appealing ad in the real estate section. "Let's drive over and check out this place in Gloyd after we eat," Kate suggested. That was also my cue to make lunch.

"Sure," I said agreeably while making two PB&Js, my specialty.

The beautiful, rolling five acres was only fifteen minutes away, and the property included two horses and a John Deere farm tractor. Having grown up with horses, I love everything about them—even the cracked ribs and busted knee I'd gotten along the way. Despite various other perks, however, the house, sheds, and barn were in mid-construction, unfinished.

"This looks like a twenty-year project," Kate said.

"I'm game if you are," I said with a grin.

I do like a challenge.

But $184,500 was more than we could afford, so we underbid by $30,000, not expecting the owner to bite. But after three weeks, Tom the realtor called. "I have a contract for you to look over. I'll drop it by tonight."

That evening I looked out the kitchen window and saw Tom pause on the front sidewalk, obviously looking for the missing For Sale sign. I opened the door before he knocked. "So, what's the deal?"

"Look at this." He came in and plopped a packet down on our kitchen table. "It's for $137,500." It was not only $47,000 less than the asking price, it was $17,000 less than our offer. "I think you should sign," Tom urged.

I paused. "There seems to be something fishy about this."

Kate echoed my feelings. "We need time to think it over."

In the end, however, we signed it, contingent once again on the sale of our townhouse.

Pyleton real estate had languished with the building boom in Germantown—a suburb much closer to the city and more commuter friendly—and three months again went by without a bite on our home. Thankfully, Dick, the seller of the Gloyd house, agreed to re-up for another ninety days.

Two months later, our phone rang.

"Carroll, the bank's gonna foreclose," Dick said, sounding desperate. "But I've figured it out: if I sell the farm to pay off my mortgage, I'll have enough left for a down payment on your townhouse."

"Sounds good to me," I said.

It was a trifecta: the bank was happy, Dick was relieved, and Kate and I were ecstatic.

Two weeks later, the settlement table was attorney chaos: papers flew helter-skelter as we were told to "Sign here and initial this box" multiple times. (Thirty years later, I still wonder if it was all legal—but I figure if it wasn't, we must have squatters' rights by now.) That confusion, however, paled in comparison to swapping houses on the same day at the end of March.

That early spring of 1983 saw DC's biggest blizzard in years. When it finally dawned sunny with a cool breeze, we hired a company to move the heavy furniture at an hourly rate—with the promise of perfect moving conditions. With friends and family helping with the small stuff, we hoped it would go quickly.

The convoy of cars, pickups, and moving van soon pulled onto the gravel lane of our new home. "Pull around back," I shouted to the van's driver.

"The ground's awfully soggy," he said with a grunt.

"Don't worry about it, as long as you can make it to the back door."

He turned the corner and stopped dead. Halfway Dick—for so the kids ended up nicknaming the builder of our unfinished home—had blocked the door with his six-wheel pickup. My movers were on the clock and I was almost busted flat after unforeseen settlement costs. Needing to get my van unloaded as quickly as possible, I rushed into the house.

"Hey, Dick. Move your truck out of my way!"

The refrigerator door was open and he looked out from it. "We'll be done in an hour or so." That meant "much later in the day."

"Look, do you want to pay these guys to stand around?" I asked in frustration.

He saw my point. "Come on kids, grab the lamps and ashtrays." His wife threw condiments into a Playmate cooler as I watched the two moving trucks jockey for position. *It'll all work out*, I thought, as I surveyed the magnificent view of Maryland's rolling farmland.

The scene that followed was chaotic. To make room for our stuff, Dick quickly cleared the living room of everything except his Harley-Davidson, which I'd agreed he could get another time. (I later camouflaged the grease spot left on the living room carpet with an air hockey table that Santa brought.) Kate and the kids unloaded our cars through the sliding glass door while Dick and his family vacated the house by way of the kitchen door. Toting lightweight boxes, his kids ran into walls and tripped over lamp cords while Tara and Russell—my kids from my first marriage—kept running into Dick's four children. A few of our boxes went full circuit. We later fetched them from Dick's house, which was our old Pyleton home.

The whole thing reminded me of our first trip to the small Pyleton grocery store. Tara and Russell,had just come to live with us. Helping stock our townhome from scratch, they filled three grocery carts to overflowing with spices, cereals, and canned goods, along with detergents, toiletries, light bulbs, and other sundries.

When we pushed the carts through the automatic doors, the rain was blowing sideways, so I ran to our beat-up Pinto wagon, turned the wipers up full blast, and pulled up to the curb in line with other shoppers desperate to stay dry. Kate and the kids made a dash for the station wagon with grocery bags clutched tightly to their bodies.

"C'mon, guys," I said, trying to sound upbeat. "Get it all in before it gets soaked."

It took several trips through the pouring rain before we had all our goods stuffed into the car. "Man, that's a lot of groceries," I muttered.

"You should see the bill," Kate said, her hair dripping wet. "Then again, maybe you shouldn't."

I backed up to our townhouse and opened the hatch. "One more time, guys," I encouraged. "Let's see how fast we can do this."

At this point, Tara had to be prodded—she didn't want to get any wetter than she already was—but Russell's lanky legs went into action, and they both did their best until the last soggy brown bag made it through the door.

The kids made themselves scarce while I emptied the goods onto kitchen counters and Kate decided where it all would go. After putting cleansers under the sink, she stood up to straighten her back. "What's all that stuff there, Carroll?"

"What stuff?"

She pointed to a pile on the counter. "That can of curry and the egg noodles. And the anchovies—I thought you didn't like them. I know I don't."

"I hate anchovies and curry. I thought you picked 'em up."

"Well, I didn't."

We stared at each other and grinned. In the confusion, we'd unloaded not only our own grocery carts, but also someone else's. It was back to our small-town store where Mrs. Shelby knew exactly whose food it was.

Although it wasn't raining when we moved to Gloyd, water played another role in the chaotic festivities ...

Our waterbed was a chore to assemble, and after wrestling with its heavy frame, I snaked a garden hose through a window and hooked it up. Soon there was a shallow layer of water in the bladder. *This is gonna take a while*, I thought, so I left to do other things.

Kate vacuumed and scrubbed the few rooms that we'd be using. Then she arranged—and rearranged—our eclectic family room furniture, which we later moved again as I piled plates, pans, glasses, and cutlery on the counter for her to decide where they went before later moving them again. (I still can't find anything years later.)

"Dad!" Russell called, sounding frantic. "Come quick!"

"Hurry up!" Tara echoed.

"Where are you two?" I asked.

"In your bedroom!"

I had to stop and think where that was.

Bounding down the hallway, I pulled up short at the doorway. The waterbed looked like The Blob, bloated far above the frame and thinned almost to the point of exploding.

So what did I do? I dug out the camera. It was a great picture.

After snapping a few shots, I disconnected the hose but forgot to turn the faucet off; water sprayed our dressers, end tables, ceiling, unfinished drywall, and the cigarette-burned carpet. It was a good time to break for lunch.

Sitting around with friends and family, we had a few laughs over the whole debacle (the beers helped). After they left, Kate and I worked for several more hours while Tara and Russell slipped away to explore the farm and pet the horses.

When Russell came in smelling of manure and asked what was for supper, I told him we'd go out for pizza.

"When? I'm starving."

"Soon, buddy. Just give me a few more minutes to rest, okay?"

"Okay." He smiled and ran off. Weary from the exhausting day, I nodded off while the sun sank toward the horizon. But soon after, somewhere in the mush that was my brain, I heard a commotion.

"Dad!" Russell yelled. "Come quick."

I rolled over on the now-leveled waterbed while Kate barely stirred.

Russell appeared in the doorway. "C'mon, Dad, get up!"

"Is your sister okay?"

"She's out front watching."

"Watching what?" Kate woke up looking anxious.

"C'mon!" Russell waved.

Tara, sitting on the front stoop, pointed across Stabletown Road to a field that was ablaze. The fire was quickly spreading, and I imagined it jumping the narrow country road and raging up our hill to burn down our new home. What was to be done?

Grab the camera, of course. It was another great picture.

Luckily, the neighbor had already called the fire department (our phones weren't hooked up yet), and the wail of fire engines were beginning to insult the quiet country evening.

Apparently, a firefighter had started a controlled burn to clear a site for his new house, and after a few too many beers with his friends, they stopped tending the fire. When it blazed out of control, he radioed for help.

Tara and Russell stayed up late to watch the firefighters wrestle down the blaze, but Kate and I no longer cared. We collapsed into our distended waterbed. Tomorrow was another day.

I hung a dramatic eight by ten photo of the brush fire in my waiting room but not a picture of the stressed bladder, which began to leak after a few nights. Waking up in a puddle of water got old, and we soon graduated to a real bed.

It was good to be home.

CHAPTER TEN

Natalia

After putting out an ad for a certified assistant, we received a response from an attractive bleached-blond doll who, although not certified, was personable, enthusiastic, and eager to learn, so of course I hired her on the spot.

"Kate, I think we've found a good one," I said to my wife after the interview.

Natalia, whose pretty name fit her dainty physique, proved my initial instincts correct: she picked up four-handed dentistry even faster than Kate had. Although she fumbled radiographs and seemed nervous about radiation (we don't put that lead vest on patients and dash out of the room for nothing), I quickly learned that the girl wasn't afraid of much and was great at everything else. For years, I took most of the X-rays, but that was a small price to pay for a great assistant.

When Kate was on maternity leave, and later when she stayed home with baby Joel, Natalia doubled as receptionist/assistant and was more than capable at juggling her duties. While taking X-rays was her shortcoming in the back, telephone etiquette was her flaw up front, which even those high-tech phones couldn't improve.

I often heard lines like:

"I don't have a clue … maybe … insurance isn't my thing."

"Listen, do you want an appointment or not?"

"Look, I'm helping him with a patient right now. I'll check with Kate when I'm not busy."

Sure, her harsh attitude came in handy with rude or uncooperative patients, but it was a little dicey with everyone else. At times she would simply hang up after a final declaration.

"Sorry, but I don't have time for this right now." *Click.*

"No, he's busy … Yeah, I'll tell him … Well, how should I know?" *Click.*

A delicate doily she was not.

I would sometimes say, "Uh … that wasn't a patient, was it, Natalia?"

"Nah, just some sales guy," she'd say with a shrug.

Well, that's okay then, I silently agreed.

The good thing was that she was calm and compassionate in the operatory and could be quite pleasant on the phone with folks she knew. But without warning, Ms. Jekyll could turn into Dr. Hyde, especially if a patient canceled at the last minute or called to say they were running late.

"Great!" she'd say. "I'll just tell Doc he's gotta stand around doing nothing 'cause of you."

Disagreeable or argumentative patients wound up with the worst appointment times—not the early morning, late afternoon, or lunchtime slots folks tended to prefer. Dr. Hyde was merciless.

But the good Ms. Jekyll would miraculously reappear—perky, pleasant, and helpful—if she liked the person on the other end of the line. If the caller was an unknown, Natalia would be polite but indifferent. Unless she was chatting with her friends or a likeable patient, the telephone was simply not her thing.

"It's the best new spa in town," I might hear her whisper to the phone.

"Natalia," I would sing out, "I'm ready to take the impression."

"I'm on the business line just now. I'll be right there," she'd falsely promise.

"Natalia!"

"I said I'm coming!" She'd shout back. "See you later, Franny."

Getting her skinny butt chairside was especially frustrating if I was treating someone on the out-of-favor-with-Natalia list. I suspect she initiated *important* calls during those appointments.

The overall aura surrounding Natalia was one of feminine mystique. She took meticulous care of herself, and she never wore the same outfit twice (Kate told me this—I wouldn't have noticed such things). When she walked through the door in the morning, she was always perfectly put together in fashionable attire and full makeup, not to mention wielding beautifully manicured hands.

I admit, Natalia spent what I thought was an inordinate amount of time and effort fussing over her fingernails. When the phone rang more than six times (my rule was no more than three), I knew she was probably busy painting and didn't want them smudged.

We seldom wore gloves in the mid-70s—our instruments had always been autoclaved, so vigorous hand washing was the standard of care. Concerned with cleanliness, I insisted that my assistants not wear any extraneous rings, watches, bracelets, or tinted fingernails. Chipped nail polish was unavoidable after numerous scrubbings, and even though the hands were clean, it might not look so to a patient.

Before entering the operatory, Natalia dutifully removed her numerous rings and bracelets but stubbornly disregarded my nail polish directive. I tried to compromise.

"Natalia, you can use clear, but that bright pink is too much."

She narrowed her eyes with fixed determination. "You cannot *possibly* expect me to go out in public like that after work!" (Note that if she was not perfectly attired for her evening date, she blamed me.)

I tried to argue, stammering something about the rules, but she merely stared at me with those soft baby blues—which now seemed to emanate an ominous hint of red.

I averted my eyes from her laser glare and changed the subject. "I once cracked a rib, playing golf of all things. Have you ever broken anything, Natalia?"

"A nail," she replied through pursed lips. Then she returned to her emery board sculpting.

The battle over fingernail paint was an uphill one I never won. But as her slender, graceful fingers did present quite nicely due to her fastidiousness, I decided it was a nonissue. Or maybe I'm just a wimp.

The only thing that betrayed Natalia's girlie exterior was this: she ate like a mountain logger.

One gorgeous day when Kate stopped by the office, I took everyone out to lunch. While dining on the restaurant's patio, I discreetly watched as Natalia wolfed down a humongous sub with the intensity of a Rottweiler. I unwittingly blurted, "So, Natalia … how do you manage to stay so thin?"

Kate glared and hit my arm.

Natalia's munching ground to a halt as a puzzled look crossed her face and she clenched her jaw.

Uh oh, I thought, *I'm in trouble now … big time.* My eyes darted every which way, looking for an escape route.

With a bolus of food indelicately ballooning her left cheek, she calmly replied, "This is my only meal of the day." Then, shrugging her delicate shoulders, she immediately returned to devouring her fully loaded Italian sub while I breathed a sigh of relief.

While no employee is perfect, and Natalia was certainly an asset, she did have a habit of reading soap opera tabloids when she wasn't "busy." Seated at the front desk with her head cradled in one hand, her light blue eyes would scan a digest's shiny pages. When I tried to steal a glance, she'd sense my presence and judiciously slide it under a stack of insurance forms.

I'd sometimes ask, "Why hasn't Ms. Smith's insurance been submitted?" or "Have you copied that chart yet?"

She'd have several patent answers ready for me:

"You (meaning me) scribbled illegibly in the chart," she might respond. (Admittedly, that was not uncommon.)

"That idiot patient didn't give me all the necessary information." (It happens, even with non-idiots.)

"You didn't fill everything out." (Again, it was my fault.)

Folks on her A-list, of course, had complete, perfectly legible charts.

One day, when Natalia went out to run an errand, curiosity got the better of me and I skimmed through one of the stories. (Note that any attempt to remove her soap opera roadmap meant risking the loss of a hand.) Here was the gist:

Lance had sired Tiffany's baby, so Steele was not the father. Readers had to wait to find out if Kelli, thrown into a jealous rage, would abscond with Lance's frozen assets from the sperm bank, accidentally switched with Steele's, a fact that wouldn't be revealed until who knows when. So, is Steele actually the real father? Stay tuned!

All of this might imply that Natalia was a slacker, wasting time doing her fingernails, reading soap opera rags, primping, and chatting on the phone with friends. But to her credit, she'd work diligently when we were overly busy; if our schedule was light, she didn't pretend to work when there was nothing to do. I silently admired her honesty in this. Overall, she was loyal and dedicated, which counted for a lot.

Natalia was comfortably settled into her double-duty routine when I hired an associate dentist. Kate wasn't quite ready to return to work, and the dentist needed an office right away in which to practice. Just out of school, Dr. Suliman Lee was miserable in her first job and hated her old boss. To help out, I funneled her a few patients, but not many.

The added burden on Natalia wasn't fair. Dr. Lee's English was marginal, and she advertised exclusively in the local Korean newspaper. All of her patients spoke Korean—most of them *only* Korean. Since Natalia spoke only English, I often heard her yelling into the phone, "What? I can't understand you. Why don't you call back when Dr. Lee's here? Oh, I give up." *Click.*

Finally (okay, it wasn't that long), Natalia said, "Hey, Dr. C. I can't take this crap. Get Sun-what's-her-name to make her own appointments." ("Crap" was the only cuss word I ever heard Natalia utter. She used it sparingly and only when dealing with Dr. Lee.)

I tried to defuse the situation with humor. "I've got an idea, Natalia. Why don't you take night classes in Korean?"

Her icy stare said it all.

Dr. Lee installed another phone line, but Natalia absolutely refused to answer it. Helping a struggling associate wasn't in her job description and, frankly, I'd already dumped a lot on her.

Dr. Lee struggled along for a year or so until she found a full-time job across town. Like Dr. Frieden, private practice wasn't for her.

Needless to say, Natalia was overjoyed.

When March rolled around, it was time for Natalia, who was obsessed with sun and sand, to get in shape for the summer. Mind you, this was not a rigorous exercise program; I couldn't picture her breaking a sweat on a treadmill, and lifting weights was out—she might fracture a nail.

No, getting "in shape" for the beach meant Natalia began making regular trips to the Tan N Glow. She wouldn't think of showing up at Dewey Beach with a sickly pallor—that's no way to show off a new bikini, so she made sure that her alabaster skin was already a deep copper brown before Memorial Day.

The first time I noticed, I asked, "Natalia, are you using iodine or something?" Her answer was that piercing, slit-eyed glare. *How could I even suggest that she'd stoop to crummy lotions!*

Some folks might look for the blooming of snow crocuses to herald spring. For me, when Natalia took her first trip to the Tan N Glow, I knew summer was just around the corner.

After her first beach weekend, she would subtly alter our schedule. As the days grew longer, our Friday workday became shorter; when she was the sole controller of the phones, not a single soul was booked on Friday afternoons. And as spring flowed into summer, morning appointments also became scarce. We might wrap up as early as 10 a.m.

As the last patient left on Friday, she was immediately out the door to avoid weekend traffic, roaring away in her sporty compact. "See ya Monday, Dr. C," I'd hear her call as she ran down the hallway.

By the time July rolled around, she began to wear a full lab coat for our "rigorous" two-hour clinical morning, her beach garb—shorts and a halter top—disguised underneath. I feared that it might someday slip partially off her petite frame, but I never said anything. Again, I'm a wimp. Thankfully, because she kept it carefully tied, a wardrobe malfunction never happened.

For most folks, the first signs of fall were short cool days when mums bloom, birds wing their way south, and trees burst forth in glorious colors. But my autumn barometer was Friday's patient load, which would slowly lengthen. By late fall, Natalia would arrive for work wearing her normal stylish clothes.

After eight years on the job, Natalia eventually moved to the shore. She did, however, continue to stop by our house for a friendly visit whenever she was in town.

Kate once asked how she liked her new boss in Delaware.

"Oh, I like him a lot," she said with a bright smile and twinkling eyes. "He's a lot like you. He doesn't get in my way!"

The tanning salon lost a regular customer, and I lost a trusted and valued assistant.

But not a friend.

CHAPTER ELEVEN

Doggone It

The Gloyd farmette we had recently moved into seemed to yearn for a dog. Both Kate and I had dogs while growing up, but we differed in our size preference—hers had always been small, and I liked big ones. "I don't want some little yappy thing around here," I said with conviction.

Thankfully, she agreed to adopt one big enough to complement our horses.

Soon after, Kate and her sister Annette went to the pound to pick up a rescue dog and were drawn to one in particular.

"I love this mutt," Annette said, squealing.

"Me too," Kate echoed. "But I'll have to show Carroll first."

I agreed to stop by the pound the following day on the way home from work with Kate. "We'll take the truck," I said, wary of her choice. "Even if I like him, I won't want him in my sporty BMW."

As the workday neared its end, Kate—who was back at work part-time—was giddy with anticipation and had to force herself to fake interest in what the last patient was saying (which was a lot of nothing). As soon as "gabby" was out the door, Kate grabbed her purse and said, "Let's go!"

I let out a deep sigh. Work had been particularly vexing, and I sported a pounding headache. But as I had promised, we drove to the county pound.

The drab cinderblock building resembled a prison—not only did a beefy receptionist sit behind a gray metal desk inside the stark lobby, but she was clad in dirty work boots, a faded flannel shirt, and grimy overalls. Her dirty-blond pigtails curled below her ruddy cheeks, and her pale-blue eyes stared hard, as if daring us to cross her. She looked like Attila the Hun's sister.

"Next!" she shouted, though we were the only folks there. Her sharp proclamation echoed painfully in my skull as she then proceeded to robotically fire a barrage of questions at us. Satisfied with our answers, she buzzed us into cell block "C."

"Be sure to follow the rules and behave yourselves," she called out.

"Does she expect us to break the dogs out of jail?" I whispered to Kate, rubbing my throbbing temples.

"Shhh," she admonished before turning to smile at the receptionist, who didn't smile back.

After passing through a steel door with a small wire-mesh bulletproof window, we entered Dante's *Inferno,* where the sound of meowing, hissing, barking, and growling emanated from deep within. Endless rows of cages were piled one atop another. "They look kinda small, don't they," I said rhetorically.

"Those are for cats," Kate explained. It was hard to hear over the cacophony, but I nodded as a pungent stench suddenly engulfed us. The smell of feces, urine, and festering wounds were poorly disguised by Lysol and Clorox. *So this is purgatory*, I thought.

"You okay?" Kate asked, knowing I had had a hard day.

"It's nothing," I said, probably looking shell-shocked.

"We can always come back tomorrow. Your call."

"No. Let's just get it over with." It seemed like now would be better than coming back. I was wrong.

We worked our way down narrow aisles of screeching,

arched-back felines and trudged onward to *The Dungeon of Damned Dogs.* Many snarled as if they wanted nothing less than to take a chunk out of my leg, which reminded me of my college summers when I worked as a mailman and dogs waited to take a turn at me. Just as I was thinking of the beast that had actually attacked me, Kate grabbed my hand and squealed, "He's down here at the far end." My headache got worse as I saw one more gauntlet to run.

The imprisoned mutt she wanted to show me was lanky and reddish, a mix of Irish setter and maybe forty other breeds—all very large. In her excitement, Kate yanked me close to the chain-link door. I rubbed my whiplashed neck as the animal suddenly leapt at me. He planted his front paws on the wire gate, which made it bow outward—and made me stumble backward.

Standing on his hind legs, he looked me in the eyes and panted. His breath was putrid, and his extra-long tongue drooled a river. Scraggly hairs of indiscriminate colors protruded from a Matterhorn lump on top of his head. But despite being one of the mangiest, smelliest, ugliest inmates in the whole place—one only a mother could love—Kate was beaming. "That's him."

I gathered what little composure I could muster and focused on the bio posted on his cage: Rusty—an appropriate name for a rogue, reddish animal. Under "Distinguishing Characteristics" the four by six card proclaimed, "loose stools."

Great! Kate and Annette picked out an eighty-five-pound dog with diarrhea.

Desperate for relief from the mayhem that surrounded us, I whimpered, "Let's adopt him and go home."

Deliriously happy, Kate cradled my head in her hands and planted a big kiss on my receding forehead. Whether it was for me or the mutt didn't really matter; with her loving touch, my headache ebbed.

We kept the name Rusty. With his friendly disposition, the

family quickly grew to love him (even me, after his runs finally abated). Rusty enjoyed our horseback rides through the woods, over the railroad tracks, often accompanied by an enormous yellow lab named Josh.

Shortly after we moved into our new home, before Rusty came home to live with us, I inadvertently left the back door ajar one night. The next morning, Kate climbed bleary-eyed from the damp waterbed and shuffled down the hall to fire up the coffee maker. I was still rolling in the wake she'd left when I heard a scream.

"Carroll. Come quick!"

Dashing from the bedroom, I found my wife plastered against the kitchen wall, pointing toward the coffee table. When I turned, I saw a humongous dirty-white dog with his head cocked to one side, ears forward and tail furiously wagging, clearing the coffee table of magazines, coasters, and pretty much anything that was on it.

To me, he didn't look threatening, but rather amused by all the commotion. "Come 'ere boy," I said, coaxing him outside with a morsel of leftover beef. He downed it in one gulp, and we instantly became good friends.

Although Josh belonged to our neighbor Dan, he freely wandered the Gloyd countryside. After we adopted Rusty, Josh would see us astride our mounts for horseback rides and fall in line behind the last horse—often a little too close. A fresh load of processed grass would frequently plop onto Josh's head, but he didn't seem to mind. Rusty, however, played it safe, constantly running hither and yon, crisscrossing the trail to disappear somewhere into the nearby brush.

Over time, something curious began to happen: Rusty's dog bowl would periodically disappear. I thought it might be the strong winds that roared up our hillside, so I bought a weighted bowl that couldn't blow away short of a tornado. But it soon vanished too. The same with a third bowl. We were totally baffled.

One day, through the bedroom window, Kate saw Josh saunter down the driveway with a brand new dog dish clamped in his steel jaw. She followed him to the church rectory across Stabletown Road where he and his undulating hips disappeared around the corner. Kate knocked on the front door of the simple rambler and the pastor's wife opened it a crack.

"Yes?"

"I'm Kate from across the street. Do you have any dog bowls over here that aren't yours?"

She smiled and stepped outside. "Lordy, honey, come look under my deck."

She led Kate to a treasure trove of stolen goods: kid's toys, doggy dinnerware, and ladies undergarments torn from numerous clotheslines. Clearly, Josh was the neighborhood kleptomaniac—and for some unknown reason, he routinely deposited his pilfered goods under the pastor's deck. Maybe Josh was tithing to the church?

Kate retrieved a few familiar items and returned home.

"Carroll, look at all these bowls. How are we going to keep Josh from stealing them again?"

"I'll think of something," I said.

Perhaps going a bit overboard, I drilled a heavy-duty hook into a bowl, which I clipped to a chain, then nailed to our deck. That bowl never disappeared.

On the rural farmette I grew up on, my father laid down strict rules about pets.

"Animals belong outdoors. I never want to see a dog, cat, or anything else inside," he said firmly. (When I was about eight, I broke that rule by bringing my Shetland pony, Smokey, through the screened porch and into the kitchen. My mother walked into the kitchen and screamed. My father came running and I received a good tanning, but I think Smokey enjoyed it.)

On the contrary, Kate grew up in suburbia with a fish tank, two small dogs, and a squirrel monkey, all of which had the run of the house—well, not the fish.

This led to the inevitable clash of wills between us. I won the first round on keeping Rusty outside (his "loose stools" quite possibly strengthened my argument). There was never any question about the horses.

I post mounted a large dinner bell to summon Rusty, who roamed free like Josh, home for dinner the same way Dad used to call for me and Lee. It took a while for Rusty to learn what the bell was for, but after one traumatic episode, he finally got it.

Shortly after we sprang him from doggy detention, a thunderstorm blew through the upper county. Flashes of lightning crackled ever closer, and sheets of rain pelted the house as Rusty, drenched to the bone, pressed his sad mug against the glass door and gazed into our warm, dry family room.

"Please let him in," Kate said, pleading. "Just until it's over."

"Rules are rules," I said. "He'll be perfectly fine in that doghouse I built for him." *Stupid dog, go into your doghouse*, I thought, closing the drapes. "It's the natural order of things. He'll live."

The following morning dawned bright and clear, the air scrubbed clean by the rain.

"Rusty's missing," Kate yelled, frantic.

I scoured the fields on foot while Kate drove around the countryside, but he was nowhere to be found. Feeling unloved, Rusty had taken his chances against the blinding rain. Kate was furious with me. Now *I* was in the doghouse.

Three days later, the Pyleton woman who'd originally given him up to the pound (possibly due to the loose stools) contacted our vet. Rusty had somehow made it cross-country to her home, and she'd locked him in the garage and called her vet, who happened to be the same one we used.

"Rusty's safe and sound," he announced over the phone.

"Great. We'll run by after work," I said, elated. Kate had been making life miserable for me.

Toward the end of the day, the lady called back. "My husband got home from work, hit the garage door opener, and Rusty escaped."

You've got to be kidding.

Of course, Kate blamed me.

The next few days around the James's household were gloomy. Kate barely spoke to me, which was probably for the best as far as I was concerned. I checked the shelters once, then twice daily. Receptionists began to recognize my voice and became irritated. The Hun at the county pound was especially curt. "Look, stop calling. You're more trouble than the animals." *Click.*

Just when desperation was setting in, a housewife down the road from us called. "This is Teresa, of Teresa's Treasures," she said. "I picked up a stray. Might be yours." She'd seen my "Missing" poster in the country store. At the end of his fifteen-mile round-trip trek, Rusty had missed our house by only half a mile.

Kate went with me to pick him up. When Rusty saw us, his tail wagged as if we were long lost friends. The tag on his collar was missing, lost somewhere between Gloyd and Pyleton, but safely back home, he hopped out of the car and licked my hand. Dogs are the most forgiving animals in the world, a lesson people might take to heart.

From that time on, Rusty was allowed inside on select occasions and never, *ever* left outside in a thunderstorm. Kate continued to chip away at my armor until I eventually let him sleep inside the house, sometimes even in our bedroom. Yes, miracles do happen. Or maybe penance is forever. Unused, the doghouse rotted away.

Shortly after the incredible journey escapade, thinking it would be a good time to broach the subject of a mouser, I announced, "We live on a farm and need a cat."

Kate shot me a cold stare. "I hate cats! They scare me."

But when a large family of mice moved into the kitchen, Kate freaked and two newly weaned kittens joined our family that weekend. Nestled inside the house on the kitchen hearth (I'd come a long way), the sisters were named after Kate's favorite TV characters, Lucy and Ethel. Rusty hesitantly walked up to them and drooled, as if we'd brought him a couple of appetizers, but after I scolded him, he realized they were also family and cuddled with them in front of the fire.

Many years later, Lucy disappeared on the very same day Lucille Ball passed away. Eerie.

CHAPTER TWELVE

Interlude

My brother and I were raised in the "ruburbs": rolling farmland beyond DC's suburban sprawl. Although lower middle class, we never lacked life's necessities; as a self-made man with little education, Dad did okay selling orthopedic shoe inserts and had been quite an entrepreneur in his day—sometimes successful and sometimes not.

However, the plight of Mom and her family was quite different.

Every summer my parents loaded our big Buick gas-guzzler and headed south to Mom's homestead, a small clapboard farmhouse in the impoverished backwoods of southwestern Virginia. With the car packed for the entire summer, Lee and I were crammed into the backseat, along with myriad dry goods for Grandma.

Long before I-81 was built, it took us forever to get to Nealy Ridge—cars slowed to a crawl through innumerable one-horse towns with four-way stops. As a result, Lee and I fought every mile of the two-day trek up the Shenandoah Valley along Route 11. When Dad got fed up with us, his beefy arm would sweep hard through the back of the car; he didn't care who he hit, as long as he made contact with flesh.

Once in Dickenson County (the least populated county in Virginia, then and now), Dad would cautiously maneuver his bulky sedan up treacherous one-lane dirt roads that coursed precipitately along craggy cliffs. My city-boy father would become more nervous as we climbed ever higher into a time warp of log cabins and log barns, outhouses, draw wells—seldom a pump—and a few split-rail snake fences that vaguely defined parched, rocky hayfields. A one-room schoolhouse was reminiscent of the 1800s rather than the prosperous 1950s.

For the most part, mountain folk didn't have cash-money jobs. As subsistence farmers, my grandparents ate the produce they grew, the livestock they raised, and the game they hunted. Grandpa did, however, earn a little hard currency by selling raw timber from his land or from the adjoining wilds (it was hard to tell where one began and the other ended).

With a much longer drive from Detroit, Aunt Aida and her boys, Bart and David, joined us for those down-home summers. Clyde rounded out the five cousins. Uncle Joel, Clyde's dad, no longer resided in the mountains though he had decided to remain in the South. He lived in a modest house just off that two-lane pike meandering through the beautiful Valley.

Our grandparents scratched out a hard life of humble poverty in much the same way as their parents and grandparents had before them. During those summers, Mom and Aunt Aida helped work the farm while we boys hiked the rugged hills and wandered the hollers, entertained by nature's playground. The time away from my comfortable home was an opportunity to experience America's pioneering spirit as a living laboratory. And, by degrees, I became a participant as much as an observer.

Although a respectful fear of big cats, black bears, and poisonous snakes was definitely in order, I was never afraid to roam those steep hills and low valleys where folks always made you feel at home. People who were ostensibly strangers, though they always seemed to know exactly who I was, took me in when I was lost on more than one occasion, feeding me before making sure I made my way home. The degenerate hillbillies of *Deliverance* were Hollywood, not real life.

Those folks living in the mountains never complained about not wearing the latest fashion or having a new car; many would never own an automobile, and clothes were often patched hand-me-downs. But they were generous, almost to a fault—true salt-of-the-earth souls. In their presence, I acquired a healthy respect for a work ethic all too often lacking today. It sounds like a cliché, but I know few people who work as hard for as little as my grandparents did. But I risk idealization; like everyone, they did have their share of faults and shortcomings.

Living in the days of yore was physically demanding, even for resilient young bucks like my cousins and me. Not much changed from year to year; we simply grew taller and the old folks older. But lots of fun was had, which often—maybe too often—involved a hefty dose of juvenile mischief.

As much as I loved those summers, I grew to realize that life on Nealy Ridge was primitive, tough, and full of hard lessons never dreamed of by my contemporaries back in Maryland. At summer's end, we always piled into our low-MPG "time machine" and journeyed back to the twentieth century with all its modern conveniences.

Out of familial respect, I recreated the honest labors of my ancestors on our small farmette in Gloyd. Feeding the livestock, tending the fields, and chopping firewood have been therapeutic for me. And whenever my kids Tara, Russell, and Joel complained that they were "bored," I'd put them to work. They've carried more firewood, limed more fields, and mucked more stalls than they would've liked. I've tried to instill in them an appreciation for the hard work needed to survive throughout much of the world. At the same time, whenever I got sick—or lazy—we never went cold in the winter. The central heat kicked in.

When I was told in tenth grade that dentists "have it made," I thought of my Appalachian relatives who decidedly did *not* have it made. I reflected on the disparity of their life struggle with that of my modern Maryland dentist surrounded by pretty girls and air conditioning.

Generations of Appalachians, stuck in a cycle of poverty, often lacked adequate food, warm winter clothes, medicine, physicians, and, of course, dentists. When my practice was finally established, I yearned to help the similarly deprived people throughout the world's most remote regions, those lost in time like the folks on Nealy Ridge.

Foundational to my many overseas treks over the years were the endless string of adventures and misadventures I experienced during my adolescent summers. I trust that the reader, in tolerating a sidetrack into a couple of them, will not be disappointed.

Now close your eyes and imagine yourself sitting on a rough-hewn, split-log bench perched precariously on a rickety front porch. Picture an Irish jig mated with an ole Virginny reel. Listen to the strumming of fiddles, the picking of banjoes, and the clacking of spoons while feet clog with joyous abandon in the sultry air of a southern summer evening ...

CHAPTER THIRTEEN

Uncle Joel

Of all Mom's siblings, Uncle Joel was my favorite. Somewhat short and stocky with a mischievous twinkle in his eyes, he was all belly and no butt (a family trait that I inherited, along with thin hair). A likable sort, he always lent a helping hand to folks who were down and out. When he and Aunt Thelma wed, they purchased a modest two-bedroom house on a pleasant knoll near Saltville, Virginia. Its short gravel driveway emptied straight onto Route 11, while the back porch faced the mountains that sired him.

The town was named for the salt mines that preserved meat for the lean Southern soldiers during the American Civil War. (I think I just heard my kids groan, "Not the Civil War, not *again*!") In the early twentieth century, two foreign industries, one British and one Yankee, moved into Saltville to take advantage of low taxes, boosting the local economy.

During the two-day drive from Maryland, Dad would pull off for lunch at one of the burned-wood signs proclaiming, Picnic Table: Five Hundred Yards on Left. While a welcome diversion from the long car ride, sliding into the fixed wooden bench was risky: splinters awaited your fanny, and if we didn't balance ourselves properly, the whole contraption might tip over backward. But overall, those picnic stops were a blast. A few boasted two tables, allowing strangers to visit and swap lies while the kids ran off steam, and yellow jackets buzzed around open trash barrels looking for jam or sweet lemonade. It was a lot more fun than an overcrowded food court.

After a day of crawling through every Podunk town with the occasional traffic light, we'd pull into the mom-and-pop Valley Motel near Lexington. If there were no vacancies, we'd go on to Natural Bridge, which boasted high-price lodging to gaze at George Washington's signature on the stone arch. (Today he'd be given a stiff fine for defacing a national treasure.)

After being cooped up in the backseat of Dad's Buick, adorned with fins that could impale, Lee and I headed for the pool, little more than a concrete swimming hole. Mom and Dad would sneak off to the lounge for liquid relaxation and a Lucky Strike. (I actually don't remember ever seeing Mom smoke; it's not that she didn't, but I never saw it.)

Arriving the next day at Uncle Joel's, we'd spend a few nights so Dad could muster the courage to attack Nealy Ridge's treacherous mountain road (the jug of moonshine Joel kept hidden in the shed out back helped).

Although Uncle Joel had heartily welcomed my father into the family, he was quick to exploit his big-city ways. "Harry, yer one dumb, son of a bitch Yankee," he'd say, "but yer all right in my book." Joel's laughing face, wrinkling high to a receding hairline, suggested that somehow it was a compliment.

"Come outside and sit a spell. Take a pull o' this 'ere *cider*, Harry. You boys grab a stick and whittle. Here's my pocketknife, Carroll."

My uncle eventually gave me that knife. I hold it as a prized possession to this day.

Uncle Joel's home boasted conveniences little known on The Ridge: indoor plumbing, a private telephone line, a Frigidaire, a gas range, and a washing machine with a power ringer. He also proudly displayed the latest Sears & Roebuck catalog on the coffee table. (For Thelma's birthday, Joel replaced her old clothesline with something from that catalog that resembled a naked beach umbrella. She complained and he got her a gas dryer.)

Always generous, Joel gave his son Clyde a second-hand British Triumph long before he was of legal age to drive it. "What the heck, he's drove tractors, trucks, 'n' hay wagons ... 'bout anything on four wheels," Joel said without apology. But because Clyde hadn't earned the money for it himself, it raised a few eyebrows among the scratch-a-living-out-of-the-soil folks and fed gossip around the local dry goods store.

"That kid of Joel's is spoilt rotten."

"How come he done buyed a foreign job? Never find no parts fer it."

"I heerd it's always got 'lectrical trouble."

"Dumb as a brick outhouse when it comes to his kid."

Dark and handsome, Clyde picked up local girls, going through them like potato chips while cruising through town like hell on wheels. In fact, it didn't take long before he totaled the Triumph. No one was hurt, and Joel merely laughed it off, saying, "That boy's sumthin' else." A few cars later, Clyde was forced to settle on a rusted-out Ford Fairlane, which he never totaled. It was the only vehicle that survived his adolescence.

Settled into a cane rocker in front of his Main Street haberdashery, Joel would shoot the breeze with any passerby. He knew a little about everything—just ask him.

Although Joel sold clothes, he could have sold anything—to anyone. A born wheeler-dealer and mountain boy who made good, Joel could hawk a Bible to a preacher man, proclaiming, "The only authentic version ta'en straight from the original Hebrew, verily spoke by our Lord His-self." Now, Jesus mostly spoke Aramaic and the New Testament was largely written in ancient Greek, but Joel didn't know that—or care. He seldom attended church, despite Grandma's untiring efforts to save his soul from perdition.

Uncle Joel was a southerner through and through. Regular customers were treated like family and given a fair price, but not the man whose forebears hadn't fought for "The Lost Cause." A Yankee accent and haughty air ensured that the foreigner would pay top dollar.

"Pardon me, good sir," the customer might say. "Might you have a sporting shirt appropriate for fly fishing?"

He might as well have taped a sign on his forehead that said: "Please empty my pockets."

The flatlander would leave in a three-piece suit with reversible vest, patent leather spats, crossed suspenders, and a linen kerchief to match the starched button-down, all of it capped off by a fancy fedora. Having long forgotten the fishing shirt, he was certain he'd negotiated a great discount. Joel had an uncanny way of making a foreigner feel special while being fleeced.

Although Joel's standing in civic organizations was solid, nurtured by a keen business acumen, everyone knew he'd been a highland hell-raiser. But as Thelma was the love of his life and disapproved of drinking, Joel swore off liquor after they were married. Well, except for that jug in the shed. (Maybe she knew about it, but he was discrete and managed to maintain the fiction of sobriety for her and the Saltville Temperance League.)

Thelma ruled the roost with an iron fist, which made the clan a little uneasy. Women just didn't do that, plus she was an Abingdon flatlander. The family was never happy with the match.

"Why couldn't that boy marry a Chadwick?"

"Or even a Counts?"

"That woman thinks she's better 'n' us."

"Well … she ain't."

The pressure might've contributed to Joel sneaking a few

belts now and again. Or maybe Joel was simply born wild. Either way, the years with Thelma were the happiest of his life.

I was only eight years young when Thelma unexpectedly passed on. Devastated, Joel handled her death by draining his jug and spending lavishly on a grand funeral. She lay in state in a side nook in their living room, the floor of which tilted strongly. The casket sat on a gurney with wooden blocks wedged under the wheels so it wouldn't take off on its own, and the furniture was shoved against the walls to make way for folding chairs so folks could stare at her and contemplate the afterlife. The dining room table was covered with fried foods so mourners could eat their way through the wake. Thelma's flatlander family showed a modicum of dignity while Joel's relatives wailed like stray cats. Mountain folk do like their *goin' home* celebrations.

After filling up on fried goodies, Bart, David, and I spent the early evening catching fireflies out back. Becoming bored, but having no desire to mingle with a bunch of old folks on death watch, we ducked into the cellar and quietly closed the double hatch overhead. Unlike at Grandpa's house, which was heated with hand-chopped wood, Joel's home boasted a coal-fired furnace in the cellar that sent heat through a cast-iron grate in the living room floor. An outside hatch led to the cellar, which was permeated by lung-retching coal dust. Only the brave dared descend into that dark, damp world of spider webs and snakeskins. Feeling foreboding and sinister, it enticed curious young lads like us.

Before the wake, Mom and Aunt Aida had admonished us, "You boys behave respectful and reverent." We weren't sure what reverent meant, but the gossip in the living room we heard floating down through the grate didn't seem so reverent to us.

"She never loved him, not really," boomed a female but masculine-like voice.

"Why on earth she ever married him, I'll never know," said another, meekly agreeing.

"In it for the 'citement, I guess," a quorum echoed, which was ironic because Thelma had never been fond of Joel's mischievous ways.

"Well, his life is certainly one thrill after another! That boy was always gettin' in ta stuff he hadn't ought to."

"Been almost *too* settled since she married him."

"He was full of vim and vigor afore her. But now … he's a gelding if ever I seed one," one biddy declared.

I turned to Bart and mouthed, "That's a horse with no balls." David looked down at his crotch.

"Nary a truer word spoken. What's he gonna do with hisself now?"

"I don' know, but he's got ta watch out for that boy a his. Clyde worries me. Reminds me too much of his pa."

Bart, David, and I got an earful while they trashed the dearly departed; even to kids, the gossip didn't seem right. "Ghosts don't take kindly to mocking," David whispered. At that, we left the subterranean haunt, sorely in need of some clean night air.

"Let's have a smoke," said Bart. *Not exactly fresh air.*

"But we ain't got none," said David.

Corn silk wrapped in old newsprint is not the best of smokes (it's probably the worst), but we found that it'd do in a pinch.

I took a long drag … and coughed uncontrollably. Bart, an accomplished smoker, grinned, his face framed by a perfect smoke ring drifting in the light of a full moon. After trying another puff, dizziness set in, and I retched something green then went to bed early.

Evening turned to daylight and the aroma of a big, country breakfast drifted down the hallway on the morning of the funeral. At first I couldn't stomach the thought of it, but I managed to choke down a biscuit smothered with gravy. Thankfully, the victuals stayed put.

Mothers have a knack of magically producing neckties, and after a mighty struggle to clip one on my collar, I filed onto the side porch with my cousins. The porch was protected by a tin roof to protect the mourners, and the dearly departed, in case of a passing shower. My eyes remained respectfully fixed on the floor, which I noticed was rotten in places and sorely in need of paint.

Thelma had patiently lain in that side nook for two days surrounded by extravagant flower sprays—not the handpicked wildflowers common at Nealy Ridge funerals, but expensive store-bought ones—with her waxy hands folded just so, a lily interlaced between her fingers. Having now been rolled from the parlor and the wood blocks secured so she wouldn't spill off the edge, Thelma's empty shell looked surreal in the morning mist that hung thick over the proceedings.

Irregular rows of easy chairs, folding chairs, straight-back chairs, and kitchen stools sat on the lawn, which swept up to form an amphitheater. Bordered by the cornfield, there was plenty of standing room for any passing neighbor in need of a good wail. All in all, it was a nice setting for a funeral.

For some unfathomable reason, I'd pocketed a slingshot and Bart had tucked a pet frog into his shirt pocket.

"Why'd you bring that wart-covered thing?" I whispered.

"Thought he might like to see a funeral. What's the slingshot for?"

"I dunno. Jus' in case." *In case of what?*

We sat with the immediate family on the porch under the stern gaze of the congregation. It wouldn't do to fidget, which might encourage Bart's frog to jump free. Not only that, but Clyde kept a steady eye that anchored us in place, his mischievous look long gone. My mind briefly wandered. *I wonder what it'd be like to use a frog in a slingshot.*

The sun soon chased away the morning fog, shining brightly on the mournful gathering. The pastor, tall and lanky and dressed in black, walked slowly onto the porch and hushed any residual prattling. In time-honored tradition, he read the liturgy—and then extensively elaborated on it. (There's no such thing as a short-winded southern preacher: in all likelihood he was self-ordained—another peculiar mountain custom—but that didn't matter.)

His opening salvo was fire and brimstone, although everyone knew what the Good Book says about sinners. As the pastor turned to look at the family, the slingshot poked my buttocks and I suddenly felt guilty about my thoughts of launching the frog. I slouched low and managed to sit motionless while the weapon stabbed my backside.

Unable to compete with the heartwarming sun, the preacher shifted gears from damnation to the assurance of Aunt Thelma's eternal reward. "She was the embodiment of everything kind and good and loving in a faithful spouse," he said as the three biddies from last night's gossip-fest squirmed and averted their eyes. "She faithfully served the church and the cause of charity." That evoked nervous coughs from the jury of three. "The community has lost a valued and much-loved soul." There it was: Thelma, who could apparently do no wrong, had taken on sainthood.

Becoming further worked up, the balding preacher reached for new heights by not so subtly bringing Thelma's wayward husband into the picture. It seemed that her every breath was divinely ordained to lift him from the gutter of satanic depredation and redeem his soul for all eternity. With stern admonitions from Leviticus, yet without a hint of henpecking, she'd led her alcoholic mate to forever swear off the bottle—or jug, in Joel's case.

My poor uncle looked grief stricken and ... maybe a little hungover?

The pastor's nasal pitch rose ever higher. Tears freely flowed, and I thought the weaker sex might swoon. The cadre of men who had gathered on the very same porch to smoke cheap cigars and toast Joel's libation liberation the night before shifted uncomfortably in their squeaky, hardback chairs. After commending Thelma's soul to eternal bliss, the itinerant parson called for sinners everywhere, especially those in attendance, to repent. Then he invited those wishing to pay their last respects, and final farewell, to do so now.

The summer sun had begun to beat relentlessly and Bart and I had long since grown tired. We eyeballed each other, then boldly stood and strode confidently up to the open coffin. Bart gave Aunt Thelma a quick peck on her waxed-looking forehead and peered at me as if to double dare. I couldn't reject such a serious challenge, so I gave her a longer smooch. Bart seemed impressed as we stumbled down the rickety porch steps and escaped into the cornfield.

Once hidden among the maturing rows, we shed those tight black shoes our mothers had forced us to wear and rolled a few corn silk cigarettes. I promptly got sick—again. Nasty stuff. As my brain swam, the sweet melodic strains of "Amazing Grace" wafted through the rows. Maybe God was trying to tell me something about smoking.

Heeding the message, I never took it up.

Joel's untamed nature hadn't prepared him to play both mom and pop, a twist of fate that left two hell-raisers to watch over each other. He became Clyde's friend rather than a father.

"Wanna go play cards and get drunk?" he'd ask his son.

"Sure 'nuff." Clyde had it in his genes.

Despite all his theatrics on the day of the funeral, the parson did get one thing right: Joel needed Divine guidance. Family and friends relentlessly worked on him until he was baptized in the creek below Nealy Ridge. He finally swore off the jug, and he also remarried, though Thelma forever remained his bride.

Unfortunately, his second wife also beat him to the grave, and Joel lost his way yet again, once more taking to heavy drinking. I was much older then and missed the kind, generous soul I'd known growing up. But it counted enough that I named my youngest son after him.

In his early fifties, lonely and alone, Joel died of a heart attack precipitated by cirrhosis of the liver.

I feel certain God doesn't want it that way.

CHAPTER FOURTEEN

Ole Lincum

Stan and Gill, my two best buddies from dental school, came to Maryland one weekend for a hike up Sugar Loaf Mountain.

"It doesn't get much better than this," Gill said with a grin.

"You got that right," Stan said, huffing and puffing as he stopped to catch his breath along the rocky terrain. Then he blurted out, "Carroll. You're a redneck, right?"

I ignored him, thinking he was just trying to be funny.

He persisted. "So, how many blacks do you have in your *southern* practice?" I stopped climbing and looked down to see Stan staring at me.

In reflection, I glanced away and realized that my practice was actually quite cosmopolitan, including my employees. Over the years I've hired a Muslim, a Jew (adopted by holocaust survivors), an Irish woman, a Pennsylvania Yankee, a Korean, and several Brazilians and hillbillies. Between Kate and me, we have quite a mix too: Kate is of Swiss-French ancestry with a little Cherokee, and I'm Scots-Irish, English, and Welsh, with maybe a little Melungeon, whatever that is. Generational Americans are all mutts. Abraham Lincoln said, "I like a Mongrel myself, whether a man or a dog. They are the best for every day."

We'd never hired anyone of African heritage, but none had ever applied; it just worked out that way. However, plenty of black folks had been patients for thirty-plus years.

"I don't know, Stan," I finally said. "I haven't thought about it."

Apparently he had. "I've got *only* one," Stan said, smugly holding up a single finger, assuming a southerner would happily relate.

But I didn't. Prejudice is a thing of the heart, not of geography. I'm happy as long as folks trust me, show up on time, and pay their bills, but our odd exchange got me thinking about my childhood visits to Virginia.

A hard stone's throw beyond the cornfield behind Uncle Joel's house there lived an old sharecropper everyone called Ole Lincum. The "ole" part was obvious from looking at him, but it had never crossed my mind that his name was actually *Lincoln*.

Joel and Lincum were good neighbors. You'd often hear Joel say something like, "Hey, Ole Lincum. Can ya split me a cord o' wood? Give ya two dollars, US silver certificates. Two-fifty if ya have it laid up by Saturday."

The wood would always appear a day early, stacked neatly in Joel's woodshed, and being an honest, trusting soul, Lincum never asked for payment. But after Uncle Joel snuck out to get his jug of moonshine and discovered the wood, he would promptly pay, always giving Lincum fifty cents extra for a job well done.

Ole Lincum's mammy was a slave of eight or so (no one knew exactly) at the time of emancipation. Suddenly set adrift in a world that didn't want her, she survived on odd jobs and eventually married. Although the new couple might've found steady work up north, her husband was afraid to go. "I'se told them Yankees eat black babies," he'd say, repeating a rumor spread by antebellum planters to keep slaves off the Underground Railroad. Southwest Virginia was all the world they knew, and being the last of their large brood, Lincum was named after the Great Emancipator. I never knew his last name.

When I was a mere whippersnapper, Ole Lincum was already about to break Methuselah's record. He had a sparse receding hairline, a scruffy beard, and tufts of white hair that sprouted from his ears. His withered fingers bent in directions fingers aren't meant to, evidence of advanced arthritis. Supported by a homemade birch cane, he walked with a pronounced stoop and wore the standard uniform of farmhands, black or white: patched overalls and a threadbare plaid shirt. His boots, fastened with frayed cotton twine, had been resoled several times. One lazy eye forever rolled about—not only did it never blink, but to look at him straight on was impossible. As for his humble abode, it boasted a wood floor, an improvement over the packed dirt with which he was probably familiar as a child.

Like any Southerner, he spoke with a guttural drawl that exuded a warmth, enhanced by a broad, toothy grin and a twinkle in his eyes (well, at least the good eye shined). Everyone, especially kids, loved his company. He was one of my favorite relatives, and I did think of him as an uncle. Uncle Remus personified.

Speaking of Uncle Remus ...

I believe he's been wrongfully stereotyped. If we discard the insulting racial overtones of Mr. Joel Chandler Harris, the anecdotes carried over from West Africa are anything but offensive. These clever yarns are akin to *Aesop's Fables*: they can be instructive or nonsensical but fun anyway—a rich heritage of sub-Saharan cultures mixed with a little Native American lore. We read *Grimm's Fairy Tales* without thinking of Nazi Germany, so why not Uncle Remus? My kids loved *Brer Rabbit and the Tar Baby* as much as *Hansel and Gretel* or *Robin Hood.*

But I digress.

While perched on a stump in his front yard, Lincum showed my cousins and me how to sharpen a blade and flip the business end of a knife into a tree. Despite his rough, arthritic hands, he could still throw like no one else, and he never let pass an opportunity to show off his skill.

One day, Bart brought over a beautiful knife that cost him a week of mountain wages.

"Whadda ya think of this, Lincum?" he asked.

The old geezer gently passed his calloused thumb down the sharp blade, checked its balance on his forefinger, then nodded. Satisfied, he grasped the tip and without standing up, whipped Bart's pride and joy at a huge oak tree. It hit with a *twang*, burying deep into the trunk. My irrepressible cousin pulled hard to retrieve his Sword Excalibur while David and I stared in wide-eyed disbelief.

"Ya'll youngsters wanna' l'arn ta throw, proper like?"

"You bet," we chimed.

"Well, now, fust time 'round put it in summthin' soft, like maybe da ground. Can't miss, 'cept dey's rocks and such might dull it." He squinted at Bart. "Only toss ole rusted ones inta the dirt. A hid rock kin chip a blade."

The old man sensed Bart's trepidation. "Nary mind dat. Da sharpenin' stone'll keep you boys outa trouble." He grinned slyly. "I heerd that ain't easy frum yer rep'tation up on da Ridge."

Eager to test our mettle against him, we mumbled, "Okay."

After several end-over-end tosses, the knife began to stick more often than not, which pleased our tutor.

Bart, ever the cocky one, bragged. "This ain't so hard."

Lincum saw the challenge and decided to make things more interesting. Although good-natured like Joel, he could be relentless—also like Joel. "Okay, Carroll. I want ya ta stand over thar and spread yer feet fer apart. Real wide like."

I respectfully obeyed and stood spread eagle. Lincum sauntered to the other side of his scratch yard and suddenly turned, whipping the Bowie knife at me. It stuck into the ground underneath my crotch. I'm amazed I didn't wet myself. (At least, that's my claim.)

"Ya done good, boy. Didn't move nor nothin'."

Didn't move! I was too damn scared to move. He stared straight into my eyes as he walked toward me, shaky from the pain of gout. With effort he held onto his cane and pulled Bart's big knife from its agrarian scabbard.

"Stay put, youngin. This game ain't over."

Game? What game?

With a groan borne of age, Lincum pushed himself upright and then pointed at the spot where the blade had pierced the earth. "Move one o' yer foots to thar."

"What?"

"Move 'em closer together, boy."

It didn't matter which foot; both were equidistant to the scar in the ground. After reluctantly shifting, my stance was now half as wide. Ole Lincum hobbled back to his starting point, turned with a speed I believed impossible, and let loose the lethal weapon.

Thud! It struck deep. I stared incredulously as the knife quivered between my tennis shoes. *Wish I'd worn boots.* Lincum ambled over and, with another arthritic tug, yanked it out. Straightening up, he looked hard at me with his one good eye. In the meantime, Clyde and Lee had shown up in the clearing, but they kept in the background, knowing better than to compete against the old sharecropper. Clyde's subtle smirk suggested that he sensed my fear.

Lincum ordered me to "Move dat foot agin."

I hesitated. *Is this supposed to be fun?*

"Go on now, boy. I ain't never missed. Well, thar was dat one time ..." His good eye gazed into the past while the cloudy one aimlessly searched. "But nar'you mind 'bout that."

Although scared, I couldn't lose face in front of my cousins. The next round left my shoes only inches apart. I coughed up the courage to ask, "When's it gonna be my turn?"

Lincum grunted. "Don't trust the likes o' you. I'll chance it when ya git more practice."

I gulped when the bright steel again buried itself exactly midway between my feet, leaving little room to further close them up. Lincum grimaced sideways and said, "Well, guess dat's 'nough fer taday. Ya'll go on and practice. T'morrow I'll learn ya'll a game whar ya kin not hurt nobody."

Bart slid his prized knife into the leather sheath that hung proudly on his belt while I sighed with relief. He punched my shoulder. "You shoulda not looked so scared."

I glared back. "What're you gawkin' at?"

"Nothin'. Jus' glad my blade's okay."

"Ole Lincum 'ill knock you down a peg or two tomorrow," I said hopefully.

"I'm gonna wear heavy boots and jeans," Bart said. He was cocky, not stupid.

On the way back to Joel's, we practiced throwing knives at a tree trunk. After a while we actually hit it, sometimes with the pointy end. Then we noticed a forlorn picnic table standing off to one side in tall, uncut grass. "Hey, let's flip it on its side," David said, suggesting a bigger target to throw at.

Two hours later, we abandoned the table to splinters.

The following fall, back home in Maryland, Lee and I shredded our parent's picnic table into kindling. Dad was furious.

Over the next few days, we avoided Ole Lincum and took advantage of the stolen time to practice. But the dog days of summer were long, and the inevitable couldn't be put off forever. Feeling pretty good about our newly honed skills, we headed for Lincum's shack wearing the heaviest boots and thickest pants we could scrounge up. Lincum wouldn't miss, of that we were sure. But what if he insisted that we throw against each other? Better to be padded.

Lee had gone to town with Clyde to fetch store-bought cigarettes, so only Bart, David, and I strutted across Lincum's yard, three abreast. Scrawny chickens scattered at our approach as the wizened old man slowly rocked and whittled on his ramshackle front porch. Lincum glanced up, then went back to carving who knows what.

"Hey there, Lincum," we nervously called out.

The rocking and whittling stopped, and he looked up with an unnerving grin. "Ya boys all ready?" Bart looked at me, I looked at David, David looked at the chickens, and the chickens looked at no one in particular.

"Sure am, sir," I said.

A black man was seldom addressed as *sir*. His eyes narrowed to look deep into our souls and saw no slight, as none was intended. To us, the man was family; we honestly respected him. But on that day, a little healthy fear was thrown into the mix. Wise and perceptive with years, Lincum relaxed and our training continued.

"Awright then. Let's have at it."

Oh God, I thought. *Why didn't I take up smoking like all the cool kids?* I could've been in Saltville with Lee and Clyde, green from inhaling good Carolina tobacco but out of harm's way. We'd spent hours sharpening old knives (Bart had made a point of leaving his new one at home) and learning their balance. But I still wasn't so sure.

"In dis 'er game, no one's gonna throw no blade at no one. Keep it real safe like," Lincum said while we breathed a collective sigh of relief. "All ya gotta do is jus' what I does. Fust, I'm gonna toss my knife straight inta da groun'. Then ya'll does the same."

"Yes, sir." It sounded easy enough.

Whoop thud. Each one of us nailed it, easy. Hitching up my pants, I strutted about with the chickens. I didn't know it yet, but Mumblety-peg is one game you really don't want to lose.

"Now, we gonna hang da pointy end from our nose and flip it. Stand up tall so's it has fer 'nough to drop. Den ya repeats da fust throw." Different, but not so hard.

The third toss from the chin was essentially the same as from the nose. Bart mouthed off saying, "This is a cinch," swaggering around the yard like a peacock one-upping the roosters.

Next, we placed the knife atop our heads, point down. By properly whipping head, hand, and weapon forward in tandem, the knife flipped and stuck into the ground. That was a little trickier, and it hurt my scalp.

As a variation on a theme, we progressively placed the point on each fingertip and flipped it. Not so bad; fingers have calluses, unlike my head. After a number of rounds, I found myself searching for a fresh spot on my increasingly scarred scalp.

We worked through all ten fingers, both palms (it helps to be ambidextrous), and elbows and shoulders. The routine stretched ever longer and no contestant could miss a single shot. If he did he was out and had to watch, humiliated, from the sidelines.

Toward the end, the knife was tossed over each shoulder with enough force to stick into the rocky soil. First David failed (actually on one of the easier throws), and then Bart on the harder over-the-shoulder throw. Lincum, of course, never missed. I managed to persevere.

Around the World was the grand finale. For this, you had to contort in such a way that your arm circled your neck and the knife stuck in front of you. Lincum demonstrated; despite his painful arthritis, he nailed it. Then it was my turn. The knife stuck and I smiled. *Tied with the master!* But then it slowly tilted and keeled over. I was disappointed but thought, *Second place ain't all bad.*

But I was about to find out why the game's called Mumblety-peg.

Ole Lincum ambled over and picked up my weapon. Upon straightening, he sported a twisted, almost sinister smile. "Well, boy. Now comes da true test."

A chill ran down my spine, but I managed to fake a reciprocal smile.

He pulled a sharpened peg—about the size of my little finger—from his overalls and handed it to me. "Carroll, you take dis an' push it inta da groun'. But only fer 'nough to keep it upright." That peg is what he had been whittling when we first strolled up to his porch.

Lincum unraveled the checkered scarf around his wrinkled neck and struggled to get down on his knees. "Put dis over my eyes and tie it 'round my head. Nice an' tight now, so's I can't see nuthin'." This was getting a little weird. "Don' be 'fraid to pull hard, Carroll," he commanded. I gave the knot an extra tug.

This old sharecropper, the humble son of a former slave-girl, was about to teach me a life lesson. He pulled a small maul from a loop in his overalls and blindly felt for the peg sticking out of the ground. His once-powerful arm raised the hammer high and brought it down with a force that belied his infirmities. The maul stamped a deep impression in the dirt, right beside the peg.

"You missed," I crowed.

"Okay, smart aleck. But da winner of Mumblety-peg gits t'ree whacks. Den da loser gots ta yank it out wif his teef." My face drained pale. Grinning, Bart and David leaned in while I prayed for Lincum to miss. *Whap.* Count two only grazed the peg. My mouth went dry as he raised Thor's hammer the third time and hit the peg square, driving it below the scratch yard surface.

"You got it," Bart exclaimed.

"Man, that thing sure disappeared," David said.

"Okay, boy," Lincum said, taking the blindfold off. "Go on now. Pull it out wif yo' teef."

As I kneeled, he pulled my hands around my back and tied the scarf around my wrists. That's when I noticed the chicken poop—everywhere. It'd always been there, but I'd never given it a thought until that moment.

Okay. Let's get it over with. My teeth attacked the crap-caked soil, found the peg, and clamped down and pulled it out. I even forced a grin around the grime-encrusted stick.

The victor nodded his approval with his good eye twinkling; he liked a good sport. Lord knows how many times he'd lost to skilled peers in the past. The filth I spit from my mouth mattered little compared to his warm endorsement.

I lost the match but learned the lesson: play the game and take what comes with grace. I continued to play Mumblety-peg with Lincum, my cousins, and friends to whom I taught the game back in Maryland. I've eaten more dirt in my time than I'd like to think on.

Ole Lincum came around Uncle Joel's fairly often, sometimes just to say "hi" and sometimes to see if any odd jobs could be had. My uncle, greeting him with a warm smile and a hearty pat on the back, could always scare up a chore or two for his white-haired neighbor. Like Lincum, Joel came from a desperately impoverished background and knew he could use the ready cash. Although Joel had become a successful proprietor of his haberdashery, he never forgot what it was like to be dirt poor.

Aunt Thelma invariably emerged from the kitchen with a basket of fresh-baked biscuits, cakes, or maybe a jar of preserves, always with a warm smile. Good neighbors, good folks.

But ugly prejudices lurked beneath this veneer of familiarity.

The truth is, despite being inside Lincum's home any number of occasions, I never once remember seeing my surrogate black uncle inside Joel's. For all the times he'd motioned to a three-legged stool and said, "Cummon in and have some hot co'npone. Sit yo'self down thar, Carroll," he was never invited in to rest on Joel's easy chair, or even to sit outside on the front porch rocker.

And the wizened old man always came to the back door, never the front, which was simply an unspoken rule. I can picture his screen-checkered visage through the kitchen door while he stood out back, patiently waiting as if white folk existed on an inherently higher plane. To my discredit, it took me twenty-odd years to realize this terrible injustice. When I finally did, it sent a chill of shame through my soul. I discovered prejudices within that I'd never claimed.

Although it was just the way of things back then, that didn't make it right, and no number of excuses will ever make it so. Honest introspection can be a harsh schoolmaster. And the pill was especially hard to swallow in light of how much I loved and respected Lincum.

So when a Yankee friend makes a sideways racial remark, I'm not so quick to judge. He's wrong but I'm just as guilty. Better to clean up your own house first. Only God's love is unconditional—a Truth that levels the playing field.

I miss you Old Lincoln. And I'm sorry.

CHAPTER FIFTEEN

Horse vs. Car

Thomas Wolfe said, "You can never go home again." But I found that wasn't entirely true when my family and I moved to Gloyd. Memories of Nealy Ridge flooded back as I looked over the sad-looking, half-finished barn and outbuildings of our new farmette, along with its two horses.

Tuffy, a chestnut-brown quarter horse, stood a comfortable fourteen hands high, and Alimony was a magnificent sixteen-two thoroughbred Dick purchased from a man desperate to catch up on his ex-wife's payments. Although Tuffy came with a saddle and bridle, Alimony had no tack of which to brag except for the halter he wore.

One Saturday in mid-April dawned overcast as gusts blew hard across the fields. But then Kate's dad, Frank, drove up our lane with a present to brighten the dreary morning: a used bridle, blanket, and saddle. All were pretty ragged, but I imagined they might look good on a nicely groomed Alimony. *Especially with me riding him*, I thought.

Confidence: That feeling you have before you completely understand the situation.

I found a cobweb-covered halter in the barn, hid it behind my back, and slowly walked into the barnyard while Alimony snorted and shied.

"He's gonna be a hard one to catch," Frank called out.

"Don't worry 'bout me," I said, boldly stepping forward as Alimony pranced out of reach. For several minutes I chased him in circles, which worked about as well as you might think. *Maybe bribery would work?* As I gently sifted a bucket full of sweet grain through my fingers, his ears went forward. Then, Alimony followed me, or rather the bucket, into an unfinished box stall within the barn. As he settled down to munch on the treat, I took off the halter and grabbed the used bridle. Surprisingly, Alimony stopped eating long enough to take the bit without a struggle.

The saddle blanket should be easy, I reasoned. But when I tossed it on his back, he freaked and shot sideways. The blanket hit cockeyed, slid off his hindquarters, and landed on the dirt floor where Alimony sprayed it with nervous-driven manure. After several more attempts, I was pinned against the timber walls. Although unnerved, I was determined to win this struggle between man and beast.

"Jus' get the saddle on 'im. Forget the blanket," Frank said, safely without the confines of the stall. I grabbed Alimony's reins while Frank continued to encourage me. "Okay, you've got 'im now."

But it didn't feel like I had him.

"Why don't you get in here, Frank?"

"Don't yell. You'll rile him and he might hurt himself," Frank admonished.

"Him? How about me?" I said.

Alimony's nostrils flared and his eyes went wide-wild before finally settling enough for me to deftly slip the sodden blanket and old saddle on his back. But as I cinched up the girth, I heard a loud *snap*; the strap had broken. In a psychotic frenzy, Alimony immediately reared high, sending the unbelted saddle into a fresh puddle of runny manure while his flailing front hooves barely missed my face.

"Watch out," Frank shouted.

"Thanks for the warning," I said with a grunt, scrambling to avoid a half ton of chestnut muscle. Retiring to opposite corners, Alimony and I warily eyed each other. The saddle was useless without a strap, not to mention pretty crappy—literally— like the blanket. But determined to ride the crazy thoroughbred, my only option now was bareback.

After he slowly calmed down—or maybe he was as tuckered out as I was—I led him from the barn and brought him alongside the fence where I handed the reins to my feather-weight father-in-law (who was a good hundred and sixty-five pounds dripping wet). Although a hefty snort from the charger could send Frank flying into the next county, I had no choice but to trust him.

Cautiously, I climbed the fence and swung my right leg over Alimony's bare back. He reared up, his forelegs pawing the air. Now, I hadn't held onto a mane since I was six, but it saved me from tumbling off and breaking a bone, or my pride. I set my knees in a viselike grip while Frank tossed me the reins—the steed bucked in circles before calming somewhat upon feeling my tug on the bit.

I wanted to just try walking during our first outing, so I ever so slightly touched my heels to his quivering flanks. Bred for racing, the thoroughbred had no inclination to walk or even trot, so he bolted. But it didn't matter to me as I galloped into the wind, thrilled to be riding for the first time in years. Riding bareback only heightened my adrenaline rush.

When we turned back toward the barn, Alimony settled into a smooth rhythmic gait as I sported an ear-to-ear grin. Then I nearly collapsed upon dismounting, my wobbly legs unaccustomed to riding. Alimony needed a real saddle—or maybe I did.

When we bought the farmette, I thought Dick's western saddle was too pricey, but I now swallowed my pride and drove over to our old Pyleton townhouse to beg Dick's beautiful hand-tooled leather saddle, paying top dollar for it. As I struggled to load the bulky treasure, along with a really cool bridle, into my Pinto station wagon, Dick declared, "Ya know, Alimony's got ta be handled with care."

Still irritated at the high price of the tack, I curtly fired back, "Why so? He's no problem." I wasn't about to tell him about our battle in the barn.

"He was jus' broke by a wrangler. Not been rid since las' fall," he drawled.

As I realized I had unwittingly ridden—bareback—a powerful, partly crazed beast that was green, a chill ran up my spine. Angels *do* watch over children and fools.

In the end, Alimony turned out to be a great ride and quite a jumper, but only when in our home field. On the trail he shied at everything: birds, rabbits, squirrels, stray leaves—even a discarded soda can. He was also terrified of groundhogs.

We eventually came to a mutual understanding: he went where he liked, when he liked, and as fast as he liked while I came along for the ride. My only other choice was to remain behind, sprawled on the ground. We stuck to that arrangement as long as I owned him.

Our Gloyd barn was situated in a side field, enclosed by an unpainted three-board fence. The smaller pasture out front, however, was defined by only a few lonely posts, irregularly spaced. In need of closed fencing, I ordered more locus posts, along with oak boards, and nailed them together with the help of anyone who happened by: my father-in-law, mother-in-law, friends, and Mom. (Tara and Russell got wise and began making themselves scarce whenever I headed out front with a hammer in hand.) Perhaps I wrangled help *too* often—while the project was in the works, my friends and family abruptly stopped visiting. My brother Lee thought he'd be safe coming over after dark, but I tricked him by firing up the Coleman lantern so we could work late.

"Folks with building projects don't seem to have any friends," the Pyleton Polo Club captain commented with a smile.

I introduced my dental school buddy, Stan, to the joy of fence-building when he came down from Joisey to see our new homestead. "Working in the fresh air's a lot more fun than being cooped up in a cubicle all day," I offered. Taking the bait—or what I call the "Huck Finn effect"—he eagerly chipped in, helping me finish the little that was left. (He proudly laid claim to building most of it.)

Along the country road, a weathered mailbox sat on a post where the gravel lane started its climb to our house about five hundred feet away. In order to rotate pastures, Kate and I led the horses across the driveway, a thirty-foot divide between the two fields. Tuffy easily cooperated, knowing that the grass was, in fact, greener on the other side.

Alimony, however, hated to be led around by the nose, despite the promise of fresh grazing. The young stud, sensing freedom, pranced through the first gate, but in the open divide he became obstinate—rearing, bucking, and generally being a nuisance. He had to be strong-armed into the front pasture, a chore that typically fell on my broad shoulders. Kate, Tara, or Russell always handled Tuffy—except for one time.

On that occasion, Alimony easily cleared the first gate but then started yanking Kate's rope. She did okay until a rope burn caused her to momentarily relax her grip. Recognizing an opportunity, Alimony broke free and whinnied triumphantly, spiriting down the lane toward Stabletown Road. My heart skipped a beat when he dashed across the tar-and-chip road to run wild across the way.

At first a dispassionate observer, Tuffy soon got her dander up and gave me a rope burn to match Kate's. With superhuman effort, I shoved the mare into the front field and slammed the gate on her hindquarters as she defiantly kicked.

"We need to catch Alimony before he gets hit by a car," I yelled, dashing down the drive with Kate hard on my heels and Tuffy running alongside the fence line within.

In the meantime, our errant equine was having a good time in the fireman's scorched field on the far hill, but when he heard Tuffy neigh, Alimony galloped recklessly back across the road.

"Good, he's going home," I shouted to Kate. Then he suddenly turned toward our neighbor's picture-perfect farmhouse.

Howard, a retired metalworker, had been born in that house and still lived there with the devoted wife of his youth. His beautiful garden was the envy of neighbors. (I'd established a small patch in honor of my father who loved raising vegetables, but my garden soon became a weed-infested jungle on the other side of the fence from Howard's. It was a *Better Homes and Gardens* before-and-after picture. I eventually plowed mine under and put in a swimming pool with water that sometimes became greener than the garden ever was.)

Alimony was now headed full steam for Howard's Eden. Without a moment's hesitation, Howard dropped his rake to help catch him. But having made a beeline for the salad bar, Alimony was already trampling Howard's ripe green beans and budding tomato plants as creeping squash vines became entangled in his legs.

There was a corn field in the far corner—not the hard feed corn common to our area but tender sweet corn—and Alimony disappeared into its neat rows, his progress marked by waving stalks. We tried to box him in, but he eluded capture by what looked like moonwalking.

Realizing that he'd have no respite to graze, Alimony raced through an undefiled patch of veggies to escape, leaving yet another path of destruction. Although I was upset for Howard, there was no time to stop and apologize. I was worried that our crazed animal might cause an accident on the road and seriously hurt someone if not soon corralled.

In perfect timing, a trash truck came along and saw our thoroughbred trotting proudly alongside the road. It jerked to a stop and a father-son team hopped out. “Need some help?”

“Sure do,” I said, panting. But the extra manpower was to no avail. Alimony, seeing the enemy increase in number, again bolted for the wide-open spaces across the road. Unable to help, the Good Samaritans continued their rounds while I fretted.

He’d been running loose for a good half hour and Kate and I were exhausted. The sun sank low in the sky, blazing in reds and oranges outlined by turquoise. I prayed that the blood-red glow was the good omen portended by sailors.

“Watch him while I get some grain,” I shouted to Kate, racing up to the barn. When I returned huffing and puffing, Alimony, who was probably a little tired himself, paused when he saw the familiar bucket, then his ears twitched forward as his eyes fixed on it.

Just then, headlights approached from the other side of the hill. I ran into the road and boldly waved my arms like a madman. “Stop!”

At the same time Tuffy, having also seen the bucket of sweet oats, neighed. “It’s time to stop horsing around and come home for dinner,” she seemed to say. Alimony whinnied in reply, set his back hooves, and leaped to run full tilt toward home. But as the small sports car cleared the crest and slowed when the driver saw me, Alimony reached the pavement at breakneck speed. He tried to stop but his slick horseshoes skidded and he hit hard into the front left fender. The momentum carried him onto the hood, up the windshield, over the roof, and off the trunk before landing onto the pavement in a chaos of splaying legs. The sound of crunching steel and breaking glass reverberated in the dusk.

Oh no! I thought. *Alimony’s killed himself!*

But refusing to stay down, he scrambled upright and ran toward Tuffy, who was going nuts. Kate, anticipating his move, was already racing up the lane and barely beat him to the gate. She threw it open and Alimony sailed through while she slammed it shut and secured the heavy chain.

"Whew! That was a close call!" she said.

Close? What about the people in the car?

Sickened by the sight of the top of the car flattened to the doorframe, I ran over to the squashed vehicle and leaned toward the driver's side broken window. "You okay in there?"

A shaky voice faintly squeaked, "Yes … I … I think so."

"Are you alone?" I tried to see through a hole in the shattered windshield, which was smashed into the dashboard and front seat.

"I … uh … yeah," he said, confused. Though he was trapped, he was at least alive.

"I'll pull on the door while you push," I said.

It groaned, then sprang open, spilling the driver onto the asphalt. I grabbed his hand and leaned him against the dented fender, giving him a quick once-over in the faint light of the approaching darkness. He seemed to be in one piece.

"Can you walk?" I asked. "Our house is just up the hill."

"Yeah," he said, shaking his head, "just give me a minute." He staggered up the steep drive without too much assistance, then looked down at his English riding boots. "I planned to ride at an indoor rink up in Barnesville this evening."

Thank God he knows horses.

With our profuse apologies, we further searched for injuries once inside our brightly lit kitchen and found only a few bruises. He'd avoided serious injury, or even death, by quickly lying down on his side when he saw Alimony coming. But I couldn't help but imagine that a few premature gray hairs might soon sprout.

"Our horse is totally responsible," I said as I gave him my

insurance info. He was gracious, and only wanted his car repaired. But after calling a friend to pick him up, he winced and groaned as he tried to stand and dropped back into the chair. "Something's cutting into my foot," he said.

When I pulled his boot off and tipped it upside down, out poured a stream of broken glass, jangling melodically as it hit our tile floor. (The old sports car didn't have safety glass.) He was probably in shock—I know I would have been after seeing a thousand pounds of brown coming at me—when we walked up the hill and he hadn't felt the glass. He shook his downturned head and mumbled, "Horses can be so stupid."

We walked down the hill and pried up the windshield frame so he could scrunch inside his car, which started and ran fine except for a screeching noise that echoed while it slowly went up the driveway. He parked it and sat down on our back stoop to wait for his friend. "Thanks for all your help," he said with a crooked smile.

He's thanking me?

The following morning dawned crisp and bright. After downing several cups of black coffee to jumpstart my brain, I headed out for work. But the smashed car in our parking lot (a halting reminder of the previous night's waking nightmare) jolted me awake in a way the coffee had not. Not only that, but it lent a junkyard atmosphere to our new, yet unfinished home. The front left headlight was gone, and the fender, hood, windshield, door, roof, and trunk were battered beyond belief. It was a miracle that anyone—including the horse—had survived, and it was equally amazing that the car had been somewhat drivable.

During our busy schedule that day, I stole a quick break to call our insurance agency. The cheerful operator patiently listened to my rambling without comment and then asked me to hold for a minute. Without covering the phone, she shouted,

"Hey, everybody, it's the guy with the horse!" In the background, I could hear the staff roar with laughter. My unfortunate friend had already called them. That's when it dawned on me how truly bizarre this was. Luckily, our homeowner's insurance took care of everything.

Early the next day, a rusted tow truck arrived, driven by a burly, tattooed driver who hopped out and sauntered around the sports car for a good once-over. Removing his greasy baseball cap emblazoned with the catchy logo, *You smash 'em. We trash 'em*, he furrowed his brow as he squatted to better survey the damage. Pulling clumps of chestnut hair from the cracked-chrome trim, he asked, "Hey, buddy. What the hell happened? Hit a deer?" He examined the brown hair in his hand. "Must've been a big one."

"Nah, some crazy horse got loose," I said sheepishly. In the distance, Alimony neighed and proudly pranced around the front field while I turned to rush off to work.

That evening the sports car was gone, but the spot it had been parked in was marked by shards of broken glass. I picked up the battered Triumph emblem that was left behind before shuffling up our back walkway (an odd souvenir, perhaps, but a reminder nonetheless). A full grocery bag sat on the bench outside our kitchen door. Holding no grudge, Harold had given us some of the vegetables he'd salvaged.

I carried them inside and announced to Kate, "I love the folks in this town."

CHAPTER SIXTEEN

Louise

With the office workload increasing exponentially, Natalia was being run ragged. Kate, still home with baby Joel, couldn't help yet so I had to hire another assistant. After much coaxing, Natalia agreed to man the front desk full-time, even though reception was not her first love.

Although I had trained both Kate and Natalia, I didn't want to train a new person again, so this time around I advertised for an assistant who was board certified; I could only chance so many root canal fires from a novice. A pleasant-sounding lady with several years' experience answered our ad. "I can stop by first thing tomorrow morning," she told Natalia over the phone.

"Good. How about eight-thirty?" Natalia was ready for some help.

Louise arrived at 8:15 a.m., a half hour before Natalia was expected, but thankfully, I was already in the office to greet her. In her mid-thirties and smartly attired, she was attractive and knew her way around an operatory. After marrying her college sweetheart and working in a large dental office for a few years,

Louise had stayed home to raise her preschoolers, a commendable attribute. When her third child entered public school, she went back to work part-time in a multi-specialty practice, learning a little bit of everything. That meant Louise could easily fill in at the reception desk when Natalia cut out early on those beach Fridays.

I hired her on the spot. Not only was she well qualified, but she had grown up in Kentucky bluegrass country and loved horses. The only downside I could find was her infatuation with Neil Diamond, who she'd once met backstage when he was less well known. She was positive that he'd written "Kentucky Woman" just for her.

On Louise's first day, I asked Natalia to keep our load light so our new assistant could familiarize herself with our equipment. (It's like a buying a new car: you know how to drive but still have to figure out which knob is for the headlights and which one is for the wipers. Even then you might panic the first time it rains.)

Case in point: When the county injunction had stopped construction in Man-Ar Medical Building, the landlord allowed me to lease his suite, which already had a use and occupancy permit, one evening a week. However, he restricted me to the treatment room with old equipment—not ideal, but better than nothing.

The first evening, I seated my only patient, Topsy, and clipped the bib around her neck. She was one of the few folks who had hung in there and followed me from Dr. Dolph's office. She probably had a proper name, but I never knew what it was. Topsy is all it said on her chart.

"Just sit back and relax," I said as much to reassure myself as her. "This won't take long."

I pushed the button that reclined the chair. Nothing happened. Embarrassed, I then tried the mouth light, but it wouldn't go on. The foot pedal didn't work the drill and the air/water syringe wouldn't squirt either. I imagined there must be a master switch somewhere, but I couldn't find it.

"Uh, I'm not sure how to turn this old thing on, Topsy," I said, blaming the equipment.

She sprang to her feet, tearing the bib from her choker chain in the process, and joined me in the switch hunt—she even got down on her knees and crawled around on all fours, something wiry older women with sun-leathered skin shouldn't do in short skirts. But she did discover a lever on the chair base.

"Here it is, Dr. C.," she announced. "I think it's a toe kick."

A tough old bird, Topsy hammered it with the leathered palm of her hand and everything came to life. With a sly smile, she climbed back into the chair. "You can work on me now, Dr. C." Topsy was a great sport. Remembering Stan's fiasco with his falling X-ray machines, I gave her a discount.

Shortly afterwards, I moved into my modern office. Despite plans to keep things easy on Louise when she first started, it became necessary to squeeze in several emergencies (I think Natalia was testing the new gal).

With both operatories filled, the waiting room was standing room only, and Kate and Louise barely had time to disinfect and set up rooms for the next patient. Natalia was willing to pitch in with assisting in the operatories, but with the phone ringing off the hook and folks crowded around the reception window, she had few chances. In short, the place was a zoo.

When time permitted, we showed Louise where dental supplies and clean instruments were kept, where dirty instruments could be temporarily stashed out of sight, and basically what to set out for the next patient. "They can be sterilized later," Kate said about the pile of dirty instruments that was accumulating in the lab. But, patient treatment could not be rushed; that was never an option in my office.

It became one of my busiest days—ever—and with virtually no time for a decent lunch break, everyone had to grab a bite on the run. Although Kate was able to help run things and assist during the morning, she had to leave by midday to pick up Joel at the sitter's.

So after Kate left, how did we manage?

Louise was the happy answer. The new kid eagerly jumped into the fray, sorting through the clinical demands as best as she could. Not only that, but she exuded a calm, soothing aura for patients while doing it.

Around midday I stole a moment for a few bites from my pitiful brown-bag lunch: PB&J and greasy chips. I was in mid-chew when Louise came hightailing down the hallway, a fistful of dirty instruments in one hand. Screeching to a halt, she looked me dead in the eye. I was horrified, thinking she was going to tell me to take this job and shove it.

Instead, she placed one fist on her shapely hip and declared with no hint of sarcasm, "I really like the tempo around here."

I nearly choked. I figured I'd let her know later that this wasn't normal, but I didn't on that day. Instead, I gave her a quick heads-up on the afternoon patients—especially the quirky ones (a little background helps healthcare workers relate appropriately to the individual needs of patients and meet their expectations). Louise listened attentively, obviously valuing my input.

While I talked, she put the dirty instruments aside, washed her hands, and retrieved a bag of baby carrots from the frig. Louise's full-figured stature belied her delicate eating habits, which were in stark contrast to petite Natalia who consumed double her body weight at lunchtime.

"Topsy, who's scheduled here around mid-afternoon, might be a logistical nightmare," I said to Louise. Although nice, Topsy could prattle endlessly about her numerous medical ailments or the latest fad in homeopathic remedies, none of which had anything to do with dentistry. If she didn't have maladies brewing, which was almost never, she might drone on about her neighbor's pet's rare disease.

"Hey, Dr. C. I bet you've never heard anything like this: Ms. Hockmeyer's cat has a big blind spot. Can't see where it's going. Walks into everything."

"That's nice, Topsy. Now, what seems to be wrong with your teeth?"

"Vet can't figure it out but still charges a pretty penny for a half-blind cat."

"Okay, Topsy. But your tooth problem is—"

"You wouldn't believe it. Runs right into the road an' never gets hit. Cat's not worth a plug nickel. Can't even get itself killed."

"Sure, but getting back to your—"

"Damn vet charges the same for a stray feral as for a good mouser."

You can imagine how I would lose focus by the time she got around to the dental crisis of the moment. And with this day's unusual time constraints, I anticipated getting further backlogged while trying to feign interest during one of Topsy's endless monologues.

Being incredibly tired during my briefing with Louise, I let my guard down. Flippantly, I suggested that Topsy would likely show off a fresh scar from her most recent operation and want everyone to take a look at it … a close look.

"With today's luck, it'll be on her skinny butt," I blurted out before thinking it through. *Did I say that out loud?* The shock on Louise's respectable, southern-lady face told me I had.

"You're joking?" she said, not knowing if she should take me seriously.

"Maybe. I sure hope so," I mumbled, embarrassed that I had said that to a new employee.

Quickly recovering her professional demeanor, Louise marched off to help treat the next three or four patients.

Not long after, the clock struck the dreaded quarter hour … and Topsy arrived. Her loud voice, raspy from smoking far too many cigarettes for far too many decades, carried above the general din of office chatter. "Tell the doc I'm ready for him," she said.

Natalia didn't look up. "Have a seat, Topsy. He'll be with you as soon as he can."

"My appointment's right now, young lady!" Topsy said with force. She had so much to tell me and so little time.

Desperately needing a break to gear up for Topsy, I retreated to my office while Louise called her back to an operatory. I was guzzling a can of caffeinated soda when my new prim-and-proper assistant came bursting unannounced through the door to my inner office marked Private. Tears streamed down her rosy cheeks.

What has Topsy said to offend this poor girl? I wondered.

But Louise wasn't crying. She was laughing so hard she had to hold her sides while she caught her breath. "Topsy had an operation just like you predicted, Dr. James."

"And?" I said curtly.

"She had a large mole removed ..." Louise's eyes sparkled.

"Not so bad," I said.

"From her butt!" Louise squealed, wiping her face. "She dropped her pants in the operatory to show me the scar!"

Topsy was never the shy one.

I ambled into the operatory, relieved to see Topsy seated in the dental chair with her pants on and the bib securely fastened around her neck. With a pleasant demeanor, I reached out my hand in greeting. "Hi, Topsy." I really did like the old gal.

She looked up, smiled broadly and, ignoring my proffered hand, pushed the bracket table aside so she could jump up. "Hey, Carroll. Wanna see my new scar?"

It wasn't really a question. Before I could answer, she'd dropped her drawers; slacks and grandma undies breezed down as one.

At such times, a doctor has to pretend to be interested and

sympathetic while maintaining a professional decorum. But it was difficult to keep my cool while our new employee cupped her mouth with one hand, trying to stifle a laugh. I took one look at Louise and, unable to hold back my own laughter, quickly turned to leave.

"I ... uh ... forgot something, Topsy. Be right back," I managed to say, exiting the treatment room. Once through the door, I practically sprinted down the hallway with Louise close behind.

It was obvious that we were going to get along just fine: our funny bones were clearly provoked by the same shenanigans. We later discovered many more traits that we had in common.

Louise continued to arrive early and work through lunch when needed. For years she remained a valued assistant—and always a friend. But my brain has forever been seared with a vision of Topsy's bony derriere.

CHAPTER SEVENTEEN

Horse Boarding

Harold, our congenial neighbor with the picture-perfect garden, told me that he had walked through the house while Dick was in the middle of construction. "Where are you going to put the closets?" Harold asked.

Dick looked clueless. "I hadn't thought of that," he said.

So after we moved in, Kate wouldn't hear of me tackling any other projects before she had somewhere private to hang her clothes.

"I'm using the back of a chair," I said with a grin. She was not amused.

As we discussed ways to get additional money for the materials, knowing I would provide the labor, Kate suggested, "How about boarding a horse?"

My dad had boarded several when I was growing up in Potomac, so I figured I knew a little about rooming a horse. "Not a bad idea. But I have to finish the barn first," I insisted.

At that point, the barn was only framed and covered in plywood, so Kate, Tara, and Russell helped me install roof shingles, board and bat walls, and Dutch doors along with three nice stalls and a tack room.

Then it was time to tackle the ladder.

Dick had begun a fixed ladder that led partway up to the un-floored hayloft. The bottom step was perfectly level with the concrete floor. (The stall floors remained dirt.) The next rung was spaced and placed as it should be. The third was *almost* the same distance from the second—and not quite horizontal. *Not so bad*, I thought. *It's just a barn*. However, as the ladder rose to the loft, the rungs became more random and cockeyed, giving it the appearance of a kid's tree house. Like in most of the house, Dick had abandoned the project about halfway up. (Perhaps the magnetic signs that read *Southern Comfort* on Dick's King Cab F350 suggested his relationship with booze—one could probably determine the amount of spirits he'd consumed at any given time by critiquing his workmanship.) I finished it, but left the helter-skelter steps as a tribute to the founder of the farm.

Now that we had a hayloft, Mr. Earl Bail, a retired county employee who lived on a nearby farm, would call sometime in the middle of July to say, "I'm cuttin' and balin' next two days. Give ya a good price if ya git it straight from the field." He always used the same line: "Jacks up the price if I have ta put it in my barn first."

After receiving the call, I'd drop whatever I was doing and recruit Tara, Russell, or Kate—basically whoever failed to make him or herself scarce. While following Earl's baling machine through the blistering hot fields, we'd pile our small pickup so high with hay it threatened to topple over while negotiating the rolling hills toward home.

But gathering hay under the relentless sun was easy compared to stacking it in the new loft where temperatures could reach 110 degrees. It's sweaty, nasty work, but at least the kids learned the true meaning of the phrase, "Make hay while the sun shines."

With a functional barn and two pastures, we were set to accommodate a couple more horses as boarders. In looking for a like-minded horse owner (the "just let 'em graze" type), I made the mistake of advertising in a large Washington newspaper. A polite but somewhat snobby man called.

"Good afternoon, sir," he began. "I am seeking a moderately priced establishment in which to board my very expensive, purebred racehorse."

Now, I'd never owned high-quality show horses as a kid or as an adult; shampooing, braiding manes, and blacking hooves were never my thing, so I wasn't sure how to respond.

I started my pitch with, "Well, we have a small farmette in Gloyd that—"

"Is there an indoor ring in which to exercise him?" he interrupted.

"Uh, no, just a three-stall barn and two open fields. But there are plenty of wooded trails around."

"And what about other horses? Might one of them be diseased?"

"It's highly unlikely," I said defensively. "We vet ours regularly, and there are no other boarders. Plus they've had all their immunizations."

The man continued. "Would he be properly cared for in the rain and snow?"

"Oh, yes," I assured him. "The barn is tight and weatherproof." I was proud of that fact. "He'll have a stall for use in crappy ... ah, inclement weather."

After his extensive interrogation (he let me know that he was a lawyer), he surprisingly expressed interest, probably because my low asking price was right. Then he naturally insisted on a full inspection of our facilities to make sure they were adequate—and safe.

On Friday afternoon I asked Tara to help me spruce up the tack room for the upcoming inspection. Toiling in the heat while sweat poured down our faces, she and I pounded eightpenny nails to make shelves and saddle racks.

Suddenly, a loud commotion, punctuated by whinnying and

scuffling of hooves, filtered into the tack room. "What's that noise, Dad?" Tara asked. We had recently added a horse for Tara and she was concerned.

"Probably nothing. Maybe a little spat to challenge the pecking order." But to reassure my daughter, I went to check it out.

Two of the horses had wandered into the barn for shade because our fields lacked trees, and Tara followed just in time to witness her new mare violently kick out with her newly shod back hooves. She caught Tuffy's hind leg, wedging it between the sturdy oak wall and the concrete floor. Like breaking a tree limb with your foot, Tuffy's leg snapped; a bloody bone protruded from the gaping wound.

Tara dropped her hammer as Tuffy's agonizing cry pierced the stillness of the hot afternoon, echoed by Tara's own otherworldly scream. Tara remained frozen in place while I chased her horse from the barn. "Go on. Git outta here," I yelled at the culprit. Turning back to Tuffy, I hoped in vain that I'd seen it all wrong.

I hadn't.

"Tara! Run and get Kate. Have her call Cherry Tree Veterinary."

After placing the call, Kate ran out to see for herself what exactly had happened. Upon seeing Tuffy, her pained expression mirrored my own feelings; there was no hope.

The vet soon arrived and led the limping mare out of the barn to better inspect her injuries in the waning light of a setting sun. After consulting a colleague in Leesburg, Virginia, he hung up and informed us that she had to be put down, that it was hopeless.

Although I already knew that, it was nonetheless painful to hear. Before administering the lethal injection, he walked Tuffy to the far side of the barn where her corpse couldn't be seen from our house. It was pitiful to watch her struggle along in such pain. Tara, Kate, and I turned and shuffled sullenly through the barnyard while he euthanized Tuffy. As a simple matter of decorum, he placed a horse blanket over her.

I had not a clue how to dispose of a half ton of decaying horseflesh, but the vet had already thought of that.

"Carroll, I wrote down a phone number for you," he said with compassion as he handed me a slip of paper. "They open at seven tomorrow morning."

Tuffy was Russell's horse. Although Tara was the more natural rider, Russell had worked hard with Tuffy to become as proficient as his sister; he wouldn't take Tuffy's death well.

It was getting late and there was nothing left to do except call him at the beach where he was vacationing with his grandmother. After our heartrending talk, I settled in for a long, morose evening. Dinner wasn't on my agenda.

Staring into space, darkly reflecting on the day's events, I suddenly realized that the pretentious racehorse owner was due first thing in the morning to inspect our safety standards, and I'd neglected to get his phone number in case something came up. *Might be a good idea to get rid of the dead horse lying out by the barn,* I silently reasoned. But the horse morgue didn't open until 7:00 a.m., so all I could do was call at that time and hope for the best.

Following a restless night, I actually awoke with a calm feeling. "Things are gonna turn out fine," I muttered to myself as I dialed the morgue, not one minute after the hour.

A perky operator answered. "Good morning. Valley Protein!"

Valley Protein? A dog food factory?

My spirit dropped when I realized that Russell's beloved horse was destined for poodle chow. I started to give directions to the receptionist, but she quickly interrupted me.

"I'm terribly sorry, sir. We can't *possibly* have a driver there today. The earliest would be Monday."

"Monday!" *This ... cannot ... be ... happening.* The lawyer was due any time, and the carcass would soon start to smell in the intense heat of July. "I'll pay anything extra," I pleaded.

"I'm truly sorry, but we're backlogged. Nothing can be done until Monday."

Despondent, I dragged my sorry butt out to the barn while a delusional thought spun through my brain. *Maybe I can hide the body.* When I turned the corner, I stopped short and gasped. Tuffy's legs were reaching for the sky; rigor mortis had set in and her morbid salute had pushed the blanket off.

She happened to be on the side of the barn facing the road, which hid her from the house but gave a clear view of her bloated body from Stabletown Road. It would be even easier to notice her while coming up the driveway. In a surreal daze, I tried forcing her legs back under the blanket, but nothing short of a chainsaw would do. (No, I did not consider it.)

I anxiously trekked back to the house, plopped down in front of the TV, and stared at the blank screen, having neglected to turn it on.

"What're ya watching?" Kate said, walking into the room and looking at the silent display.

"Nothing. Go look out by the barn."

She soon returned, her face reflecting my own disbelief. "Whadda we do?"

"Wait ... I guess."

Midmorning came and went. Lunchtime passed.

Figuring the racehorse guy got lost, I wandered outside and saw a Jaguar XJ16 slowly backing down our driveway. He'd finally found our house, but after a quick look around, and without getting out of his car, he probably figured his horse wasn't safe here.

I sighed and was moseying back to the house when the telephone rang. I dashed in and picked up in time to catch Valley Protein's driver.

"I'm thinkin' 'bout coming tomorrow," he said in a raspy voice. "Have ya'll got a Catholic church nearby?"

"Sure do," I said. "There's a nice country church a few miles up the road." *A church graveyard for Tuffy might be nice*, I thought to myself.

"That'll work out. See ya tomorrow," he said.

I thanked him but hung up before telling him where to find the body. Then I reckoned that all he had to do was look toward the barn and follow his nose.

Early on Sunday morning, a heavy-duty pickup announced its arrival with a roar as black diesel smoke spewed from its chrome stack. Out climbed a burly man in faded overalls, Wellingtons, a threadbare flannel shirt, and a camo baseball cap perched high on his forehead. A cigarette dangled from one corner of his mouth.

Walking out to greet him, I was hit by the rancid odor of decaying meat; he'd already picked up a dead cow, black with hungry flies. *Maybe the smell of tobacco helps him get through the day*, I reasoned. Noticing that vultures, or some other scavengers, had attacked the cow, mangling it to shreds, I quickly examined Tuffy who was thankfully still in one piece.

The truck he drove had been modified for the purpose—when opened, the tailgate could be lowered by hydraulics. The dead animal could then be ignobly dragged onto it by means of an evil-looking hook attached to a steel cable wrapped around a motorized winch.

Desensitized and indifferent to the task, the driver cheerfully chatted away as he placed a leather harness around Tuffy's torso, attached the hook, and pulled a lever on the side of the truck bed. The winch groaned.

"Can't tell ya how hard it is to keep help ... that's why we're backed up," he said, pulling a second lever to activate the tailgate, flipping Tuffy's body against the cow with a sickening *thud*. "Last guy quit after jus' a week."

Go figure.

Assuming he'd already attended Mass, I casually asked, "Any more stops, or are you going straight back to Hagerstown?"

"Nope. I'm headin' up to *your* St. Martha's," he said with a grin.

I had a nightmarish vision of him pulling into the parking lot with this ghastly load as smiling parishioners, dressed in their Sunday finest, held the hands of tykes who would sniff the pungent air while adolescents laughed at the welcome diversion. I pictured the driver hopping out with a smile and announcing, "Good morning y'all. Dr. Carroll James of Gloyd sent me!"

Kate and I decided against boarding horses.

One morning, a couple years down the road, I saw a neighbor coaxing three horses into our front field with a bucket of grain.

"What's up, Brenda?"

"Your horses got loose. I knocked on your door but no one answered," she said with a smile. "Thought I'd just put 'em back."

"They're not my horses," I said. "But go ahead. We'll try to find out who they belong to."

"I'll ask around too," Brenda said, pushing the last one through the gate.

Kate located the owner who didn't know they were missing—and no longer wanted them. We kept the large gelding, which Russell named Sundance.

As time went on, I'd sometimes double up on Sundance with Joel, but as Joel grew, it got a little cramped for the two of us, especially on trail rides. By age five, he needed a horse of his own.

Soon after, I saw a notice in the country store. A lady on a distant farm was looking for a good home for their Welsh pony, Dolly, after her teenage daughter had outgrown her. At twenty-eight years old, Dolly had a great disposition and was perfect for Joel, who soon became quite attached to her. (I conveniently neglected to mention Tuffy's fate during the interview.)

Another year passed and a beautiful spring morning

dawned. The smell of honeysuckle wafted on a gentle breeze, and lovebirds chirped as Kate and I prepared for a ride through the ancient forest across the railroad tracks. We'd taken that Monday off from work, and the weather had cooperated perfectly.

After putting Joel on the school bus, we caught our mounts and led them into the barn. Dolly followed us inside but was acting weird, pawing at the ground and skull-butting us. It was so out of character that I soon became concerned and stopped grooming Sundance to give Dolly a once-over, but I couldn't see anything wrong.

"Maybe age is catching up with the old gal," I suggested to Kate. "We'll phone the vet if this keeps up. But right now I wanna get going and not waste the day." Imbued with a little bit of Nealy Ridge self-sufficiency, I was never quick to summon the horse doctor.

Kate and I returned home from our long trail ride, exhausted but happy. Joel's pony greeted us like her old self, nuzzling affectionately for a treat, which confirmed my decision not to call the vet.

After a quick breakfast the following day, I headed out for the office and noticed vultures circling. Dolly's legs were sticking straight out while a swarm of flies buzzed around her torso, now an all-too-familiar sight around the James's homestead. As if to announce, "I told you I was sick," she'd expired right next to the fence that bordered the lane.

I couldn't go to work before having a father-son talk with Joel, so I backed the car up our gravel driveway. He was almost ready to leave for school, but I took him back into his room and sat on the edge of the bed.

"Listen, buddy. Dolly passed away last night," I said with compassion. "I'm really sorry, but she was quite old. It was just her time."

He slightly nodded, taking the news pretty well. With renewed confidence, I continued, "She wasn't acting herself yesterday. I was gonna call the vet, but she died during the night." Seemingly unfazed, he stood and finished getting ready for school. I gave him a big hug.

I knew exactly who to call before I headed out of the house a second time. The same pleasant receptionist at Valley Protein promised that a driver would pick up the corpse before Joel got home from school.

"Well, will you look at that," she exclaimed. "You're already in our computer."

Maybe I should put them on speed dial, I mused.

The dog food company, true to its word, picked up Dolly's carcass before I got home that evening. *Thank God for small favors.* After putting my briefcase down in the kitchen, I kissed Kate and asked, "How did Joel take it when he saw his dead pony lying there by the driveway?"

"He was fine, holding my hand as usual while we walked down to the bus stop," she said with a sly smirk that unnerved me. "He hesitated briefly when we came to Dolly's body, but then he picked up the pace and marched on down without a word."

Although I had a sinking feeling, I said nothing.

Kate continued. "After the bus came, I gave Joel a quick peck on the cheek. Then he hopped aboard."

I gave Kate the *yeah ... then what?* look.

"He paused beside the driver, then he turned to face the crowd of kids and said, 'My horse is dead because my father wouldn't call the vet!'"

I closed my eyes with a grimace as Kate went on to detail how the elementary-school-age kids plastered their faces against the dusty windows to get a glimpse of the carcass, which was easy to spot with its legs extended in that morbid salute my family was now so familiar with. *Maybe we could adopt that as our farm logo,* I thought.

My reputation became mud at the elementary school with kids, bus drivers, teachers, counselors, custodians, and concerned parents of the PTA. I definitely wasn't looking forward to seeing my son that evening. Kate now had to comfort *me*.

I went into Joel's bedroom and tried to explain myself, but he simply shrugged, having already moved on. After proclaiming his dad's negligence to the whole world, he never again brought it up. Great kid.

After that incident, though, I did become a little quicker to call the vet when something was amiss with one of our many animals.

Note: No horses passed away during the writing of this story.

CHAPTER EIGHTEEN

To Russia with Love *or* Once Upon a Time in the Soviet Union

"Our church is seeking volunteers for a delegation we're sponsoring for a two-week junket to the Soviet Union," Pastor Winston, his Adam's apple bobbing within his slender neck, announced from the pulpit. Tall and gangly, with a high forehead that had outgrown his comb-over, he was Gloyd's own Ichabod Crane.

I'd always been fascinated with Russia: its sheer size, epic literature, and grand music. Everything's *bolshoi*—big. Lost in a Russian novel, I'd envision myself astride a mighty steed, racing across snow-covered steppes while a lonely village materialized in the crystalline distance.

I eagerly volunteered and went to a small shop near Washington's State Department to have a photo taken for my visa. A jolly rotund lady sat me on a stool. "Now, honey, don' you be smilin' for them Russians. They jus' want frowns." The picture on my passport, which I lived with for ten years, resembled Boris Badenov's scowl.

In 1988, the fifteen delegates of US-USSR Bridges for Peace teamed up to try to reduce Cold War tensions on a grassroots level. Previous teams had included civic groups, educators, churches, students, etc. Amnesty organizations need not apply; they were unwelcomed in the Soviet Union.

My team, which was made up of members from around the Beltway, gathered with former delegates to hear their experiences and sample traditional Russian cuisine.

"Talks will be strictly controlled by the Soviet Peace Committee," Steve, our straight-laced, no-nonsense coordinator explained. "*Pravda* means 'truth' and *Izvestia* means 'news.' A popular joke states: 'In the *Izvestia* daily, there's no pravda, and no izvestia in *Pravda*.'" That was as lighthearted as ever Steve got.

The night before we were scheduled to fly out, Kate made a great last supper for me: shrimp cocktail, salad, steak 'n' potatoes, warm rolls with real butter, and lemon meringue pie with a scoop of Breyers (I often thought longingly of that meal over the following two weeks). In the excitement—or trepidation—neither Kate nor I could sleep. The heavy meal certainly didn't help.

That morning, the entire team drifted red-eyed into Dulles Airport. Kate grabbed everyone's camera for group shots, and with fifteen straps wrapped around her wrists, draped over her shoulders, and choking her neck, she looked like a member of the *paparazzi*.

"Aeroflot Flight 807 is now boarding at gate D-6," announced a loudspeaker.

After many tearful farewells, we headed for a forbidden land, our nation's number-one enemy. I faked a smile as I hugged Kate good-bye. This would not be a vacation.

The Ilyushin craft was a sad copy of a Boeing 727, designed for much shorter hops than this twelve-hour marathon. And the

Russians had packed in a couple extra rows, which gave me a new appreciation for my short, Scots-Irish legs.

We flew through night and into the dawn. Moscow's distant rooftops reached skyward through the early-morning haze as we descended. I could barely contain my excitement when we touched down at Sheremetyevo International Airport. Then I saw the young customs agents armed with automatic weapons. One guardian of the Motherland stared at my passport and then at my face ... repeatedly. While several others scrutinized our baggage—for hours—Lorne, an elderly church administrator, exclaimed, "Well, Toto, we're not in Kansas anymore!"

We hopped a charter bus to the Hotel Ukraina, a dark, foreboding structure that was one of seven such Stalin buildings. Four harsh towers punctuated its corners while the center spike stabbed starkly at an overcast sky. Dark clouds swirled briskly about the black spires, accentuating an Evil Empire effect.

While more armed guards inspected our papers at the entrance, the nine-foot-high door slammed shut behind us, the *thud* echoing through the cavernous lobby. Stony-faced desk clerks in wire-rim glasses stood behind protective glass. It felt like a visit to see Uncle Vanya, imprisoned for bootlegging vodka.

Clippity-clop ... clippity-clop. A large lady in a plain suit, heavy platform heels, and hair pulled back in a tight bun announced, "Passports, pleeeaze." When she had to tug on mine (I hate giving up my passport and kept a grip on it), her plastic smile disappeared. But then I thought about all those persuasive AK47s and my hand relaxed. With a huff, she snatched it, never to be seen until we left two weeks later.

The enormous, yet crammed elevators reeked of body odor and decayed teeth. Semi-fresh air washed in when the doors opened, only to again become oppressive as they closed.

My roommate, Jamie, and I spilled onto the twenty-sixth floor, where a beefy hall monitor short-stopped us with a jerk of her head. Small blocks of wood, chained to old-fashioned skeleton keys, hung above a metal desk against the wall. She perused our paperwork, muttered something in Russian and, with a glare that implied, "I dare you to cross me," handed Jamie a key. Unlike the bespectacled clerks downstairs, she wasn't protected by bulletproof glass—she didn't need to be.

Wanting to escape her glare as quickly as possible, Jamie hurried to our door and fiddled with the lock until it creaked open into our Spartan quarters: two tiny beds and one bedside table. Jamie's six-foot-four frame hung over the end of his bed (awkward, but at subsequent hotels we didn't always get separate beds, which was even more awkward). The shower lacked a curtain and the toilet lacked water. Wondering how it worked, I pushed the knob and water shot from the back and across a porcelain island in the middle. Luckily, flushing mostly worked.

Jamie was a young Episcopal priest with short-cropped hair who taught Russian history at DC's St. Alban's school. As anxious to see the sights as I was, despite the matron's directive—"Wait in rum; slep till meal. Feel beeter."—we accepted an invitation to join a two-kilometer sightseeing stroll to Red Square.

Paul, a team member from Philadelphia and Yugoslav expatriate who had written a book on Christian-Marxist dialogue, had been to Moscow several times and led the expedition. Including Jamie and me, six team members went along. We grabbed our pass to reenter the hotel—another wooden block with Cyrillic writing and a key attached—and headed out.

During our walk, several brazen young Muscovites kept pace beside us. One of them said to me in a low tone, "I like … would to trade shoes … rubles for sneakers." He gazed down at my feet. "Favorite, she is Nike." *No surprise your favorite is the brand I'm wearing*. But I didn't want to be arrested for illegal trafficking my first day in Mother Russia, so I said, "Nyet."

Shortly after passing the Arbat neighborhood, I exclaimed, "There it is!"

Looming large, as if from an epic Russian novel, were the

rust-colored walls of the Kremlin, an imposing backdrop to Red Square. To the right was Lenin's Tomb, and opposite were the colorful onion domes of Saint Basil's Cathedral. The Tomb of the Unknown Soldier brought to mind the horrors of WWII—even Stalin curtailed his religious persecutions. Cathedral Square's churches, however, were now just museums.

In 988 AD, Vladimir the Great forced a mass baptism in Kiev's Dnieper River. Church membership was mandatory, which set the tone for the twentieth century, when only party members could get a decent job or flat. In the interim, however, the Orthodox Church had become the soul of the people, sustaining peasants during the misguided politics of Potemkin the Charlatan, Rasputin the "Mad Monk," and sadistic rulers such as Ivan the Terrible and Father Joe's kulak genocide.

Despite the biting wind that whipped through the narrow medieval streets and swept down broad boulevards, our spirits weren't dampened. Before perestroika and Gorbachev, we'd never have been allowed to leave the hotel and roam so freely without an escort.

Back at the hotel, after I took a lukewarm—which trickled to cold—shower, Jamie tossed me a towel. "Have one of these flimsy rags full of holes." I laughed (but he was right), then I dressed and we went downstairs to a sumptuous meal in an elegant dining room. When we returned to our room, we had a clean stack of extra-thick bath towels. Our rooms must have been bugged!

After a sound night's sleep, our first meeting was with the Moscow Peace Committee, and like all subsequent conferences, it was carefully choreographed: different rooms and faces but always the same rhetoric.

"Welcome to worker's paradise."

"Plenty to eat?"

"Best food in world. Maybe France better?" *A concession.*

"Same for all comrades."

"Religious freedom number one socialist agenda," a soviet might say to play to our team's sensibilities.

"Ninety percent people vote in election."

"Yes, unlike capitalist West," another soviet would say to reinforce that. Sadly, he was right on the money. But when Jamie pointed out that we had a choice of candidates, their English would degenerate. "No understand."

"All peoples vote *da* or *nyet*," proclaimed one irate apparatchik. (Of course, a vote of *nyet* could cost you your job, housing, or worse.)

Day after day, boring soliloquies extolled the virtues of the worker's paradise, which became parroted noise. Only the intermittent sightseeing rejuvenated us. As honored guests, we took a special Kremlin tour and saw the Moscow Circus, which is best experienced in Moscow. At the Bolshoi Opera House, we saw an opera based on a German fairy tale, written by a Frenchman, and sung in Russian. I dozed off but awoke to see the hero die and recover—several times—before wailing something in Russian and finally succumbing. A few team members awoke at the final applause. Jamie, fluent in Russian, enjoyed the whole thing.

Isolated from the outside world, we were without access to international telephone service. What's more, Soviet TV showcased homeless Yanks sleeping on subway grates, or insensitive Brits eating roast pork while the proletarian world starved. Kate received my one telegram only the day before I got home. To cut exorbitant costs, I abbreviated it: "Cold as *WT*." Her friend deciphered it and they howled laughing.

After a week in Moscow, we flew to Lvov in Ukraine, an ancient city of intricate stone architecture not far from the Polish border. Soaring spires, flying buttresses, gargoyles, and friezes of saints and cherubs adorned medieval cathedrals, where graveyards filled with crypts of long-forgotten dukes and duchesses bordered parks that showcased mounted heroes. Quaint shops lined narrow cobblestone streets. I almost expected to see Pinocchio skipping along with Geppetto trudging not far behind.

One morning, I took a short walk alone in a picturesque park near our hotel, where I was pelted by brisk gusts in the cold gray drizzle. But the locals seemed oblivious of the dreary weather as they hurried off to work. I watched as a babushka held the hand of a small boy, probably her grandson, who marched along in bright red galoshes. Spotting a puddle, he suddenly pulled loose and jumped in with a splash of delight. Grandma scolded and lightly smacked his butt. He whimpered but quickly recovered and skipped down the winding path. Even at a distance, I saw a slight twinkle in the old lady's eyes. It's what little kids do; they jump in puddles. And what grandmothers do—softly discipline.

I turned introspective. *This is ground zero. Nuclear warheads (Armageddon purchased with my tax dollars) are targeting them … and me.*

Sarah, my fellow Gloyd delegate who was blond, stout, and a little younger than me, suggested that we start taking morning walks together to sharpen our senses for the day's work. One day we wandered too far afield and got turned around—a little scary in a place where few folks spoke English and an oppressive regime fostered distrust.

"It's getting late, Sarah. We should get back," I suggested.

"Yeah, I'm ready for breakfast. But which way?"

"I think it's this way," I said with an assurance I didn't feel.

The narrow street, lined with cast-iron street lamps, curved and reached a dead end. A stylishly dressed woman emerged from the arched doorway of a townhouse and hurried down the worn stone steps. I waved to her and asked for directions with a few memorized Russian phrases.

In British-accented English, she emphatically announced that she was *not* Russian. "I am Polish, from an old family here in Lviv. We seldom speak Russian."

"Lviv" was the city's Ukrainian name. Embarrassed, I muttered, "Sorry. I don't speak Russian either."

"I could tell."

"We're Americans looking for the Hotel Lvov," Sarah said.

At that her round visage brightened. Americans were rare around here. "The enemy of my enemy is my friend." But we didn't feel like anyone's enemy; just lost souls in need of a friend.

"It's not far. Go two streets down and make a left. You'll see it," she said, pointing.

"*Spasiba* ... uh ... thanks," I said hesitantly.

"Good luck ... and welcome to *Lviv*," she said with a grin, rushing off to work. It was the first heartfelt welcome we'd gotten in the USSR.

Sarah and I briskly walked along an eight-foot-high stone wall that enclosed an Orthodox monastery—one not destroyed by the Bolsheviks—with folks streaming into an ancient entryway, young and old, male and female. We elbowed through the crowd for a glance at the cathedral within, and then squeezed back upstream and out the gate.

"Let's see if Kevin is back from his morning run," Sarah said with a knowing smile.

Kevin was a lanky fitness nut who had smuggled a duffel bag full of benign religious literature into the USSR—Sunday school lessons, coloring books, etc.—that were considered illegal propaganda with steep penalties in the Soviet Union.

Back at the hotel, I pounded on Kevin's door. He opened it a crack, a bath towel wrapped around his waist. "Hey, what's up, Carroll?"

"We want to take your duffel to a crowded church nearby," Sarah said.

"Great. I'll be right there." Kevin had been waiting for such a time as this.

We were soon crammed inside St. George's Cathedral—

standing room only—inching along the back wall while subtly gesturing to our pamphlets. The congregants turned away and pretended not to notice us.

Finally, a young woman hesitantly peeked at my tract written in Cyrillic with a picture of Jesus on a hillside, possibly the Sermon on the Mount. "Blessed are the Peacemakers ..." Her eyes shifted nervously before she snatched it, keeping it at waist level. She slowly looked down and her hands began to quiver, then a smile spread across her pale face, framed by a lightweight scarf. She glanced up and whispered, "*Spasiba bolshoi.*" Thank you very much.

She quietly passed it to a friend who nervously nodded toward the duffel. Kevin gave her a booklet with Noah's Ark on the cover, which she showed to her three stair-step children who gawked at the colorful animals filing in two by two.

As the brochures were quietly passed around, the hushed tones became progressively louder and there was a sudden rush toward us. In the crush of a few electrifying, almost terrifying, minutes, our entire stash was gone. With our duffel empty, we headed for the door, receiving myriad double-cheek kisses, hugs, and handshakes. The spiritual hunger we'd been told didn't exist in the USSR—but clearly did—blessed us far beyond our simple gifts.

A couple days later, our team boarded an evening train for Kiev. "The Soviets are afraid we'll spy on the countryside," Steve explained as the sun set. The tiny communal bathroom, with a waterless sink and toilet that opened directly onto the tracks, was in an adjoining car; the coupler had to be crossed to access it—a little exciting. Despite the breaks screeching at every village and the fact that we were crammed into triple berths, Jamie and Paul slept well. Not me.

In the frigid morning air, after eight jolting hours, we climbed down to the Kiev station's platform and stretched our legs. As the sun rose brightly, someone began singing, "*Oh what a beautiful morning* ..." All of the Americans spontaneously joined in, which brought disapproving looks from somber Soviets.

After a tortuous bus ride, we milled around on the sidewalk outside our hotel while Steve checked in. A youngish woman, neatly attired in a business suit, boldly struck up a conversation with Paul. After learning her name was Tanya, he asked the group, "Who's up for going to a Pentecostal service with Tanya?"

Pentecostals in the USSR? "I'll go," I said.

"Me too," echoed those who decided to forgo a nap and shower.

Each of the three rusting cabs we hired sported a cracked windshield, missing at least one wiper blade (in the rigidly controlled economy, wiper blades were a low priority). In light of that, the driver would reach his left arm outside to smear dew from the windshield whenever he slowed—never stopped—for red lights. The bald tires squealed every time he swerved.

"Why do you attend church so far away?" I asked Tanya, who had squeezed into the front seat beside me.

"No one see me. Underlings love snitch," she said in broken English. A good job, nicer flat, and more vacation time were perks she could easily lose as a churchgoer.

The cab skidded to a halt outside a drab, rectangular building that looked like a factory. *Maybe they used to make wiper blades here*, I mused.

"Where's the church?" I asked.

"Here. Please to come in," said Tanya. Although it was already packed with parishioners, our bold hostess forced her way through the throng, leaving some of us behind in the process. From the center aisle, I saw team members scattered throughout, holding their cameras high to take blind shots of the crowd.

One elderly gentleman with random wisps of white hair sprouting from his head tried to talk to me, at first in Ukrainian and/or Russian, then maybe Polish, German, or French. Finally, he tried English.

"Where from?"

"America," I said.

That was a showstopper. People turned their heads while excited chatter spread through the cavernous ex-warehouse. They smiled and patted our backs as ushers came to lead us forward. Folding chairs magically appeared in front of the altar where I was embarrassed to sit while so many had to stand.

Midway through the three-hour service, the pastor asked us to sing a hymn. To the delight of the congregation, we belted out a reasonable rendition of "Amazing Grace" before the kids came forward for their children's lesson, which circumvented a law against Sunday school.

On the way back to the hotel, I noticed an army of babushkas sweeping Kiev's streets with straw brooms. I asked Steve, "Is this make-work?"

"Yes and no," Steve answered. "After the Chernobyl disaster, the city was sealed off, until recently. The cleanup is to reassure the populace, and foreigners, that any residual radiation is being controlled."

That was about the time I started to lose my hair.

The following morning we met with the Kiev Peace Committee, which touted the deep fraternal love between Ukrainians and Russians—blatantly false—while television cameras trained on one Soviet who berated the West for distorting Soviet history. Jamie, who had a PhD in Russian history, turned bright red, stood up, and planted his white-knuckled fists on the table.

"If you'd stop altering your history every time the Politburo changes, maybe we could get it straight," Jamie said forcefully.

The interpreter hesitated to translate and after he did, the apparatchik scowled. Everyone shuffled nervously until Jamie sat down. The Soviet head honcho made some lame joke and the meeting again became rote propaganda.

The Kiev Committee canceled our second meeting, substituting it with a meeting of university students who were tight-lipped (college was a precarious privilege). During a recess, while everyone strolled aimlessly through the university's marble hallways, several English-speaking students struck up muffled one-on-one conversations.

"I like pick own job—teaching—but must study science," said a studious-looking sophomore.

"I can't travel West. Parents in weapons development," said another who glanced nervously around. "Not permitted outside country."

The monolithic communist wall had begun to show a few cracks.

Another night train delivered us to Moscow. Compared to its cramped berths, the Hotel Ukraina was like Shangri-La. Although we'd been forewarned of depression sometime during our mission, it hit me hard that drizzly morning. I slowly dragged myself out of bed after Jamie went to breakfast and rang our leader to tell him I was sick. It wasn't really a lie.

During the meetings I skipped at Izvestia and Pravda, Paul was approached by a dissident named Yuri who arranged clandestine meetings for any who wished to meet with the underground. After shaking the gloom—and wanting our mission to be more meaningful—I volunteered along with five others, including Paul. It was a little risky as we'd miss the nighttime festivities.

Six of us, including Yuri, piled into one cab, which after about forty-five minutes stopped on a decaying side street. With trepidation, we climbed out and followed our guide past an unmarked white van sporting a whip antenna. Inside, a video camera was aimed at the decrepit apartment building we were heading to, but as we passed by, it suddenly swung around to follow our progress. There was no pretense of secrecy.

A chill went up my spine. *This is nuts.*

The apartment building's crumbling archway led to a passage poorly lit by a dirt-encrusted bulb suspended by a threadbare wire. Paint peeled from the walls and the metal staircase was rusted. Incongruously, a new electric cord coursed up the stairwell into the first apartment on the right. Nervously, we climbed up to that flat.

Yuri knocked twice and entered without waiting for an invitation. He exchanged kisses with a thin, middle-aged man named Andropov with a burly beard who was recently released from the Gulag.

As we crowded into the one-bedroom apartment, I noted that it seemed colder inside than out. In the kitchen, Andropov's roundish wife sat on a three-legged stool beside a small table. A youngster wearing oversized hand-me-downs clung to his mom's legs and looked up in wide-eyed wonder. Born soon after his dad disappeared into the prison camps, the disheveled boy had no early memories of him.

As we looked around, we saw several older kids lounging about in ill-fitting clothes. Propped against a wall or sitting on counters, they eyed us suspiciously. The eldest, his head shaved, stood with legs slightly apart ready for a brawl.

After introductions, I inquired about the new wire in the stairwell. "Did you just get a telephone?"

"For listening device," Andropov replied nonchalantly.

Now, I'm under no illusions that my country is one hundred percent compliant with constitutional guarantees—it's not—but that would make headlines in the United States. Not in the USSR.

Andropov's wife sobbed softly. When asked what was wrong with her, Yuri replied, "Because you here." Andropov gently patted her shoulder, but she would not be consoled, convinced that the men in the van would drag her husband off to prison as soon as we left. Under perestroika it was unlikely that we'd be arrested, but the dissident was taking quite a chance meeting with us.

Andropov had suffered the horrors of labor camps for seven long years. When Kevin asked what crime he'd been charged with, he declared, "Imprisoned for illegal foreign contact." *Exactly what he's doing now.*

But despite the risks he took, Andropov was one of the unsung heroes who changed the world. He was later featured in a *US News and World Report* article, but he still hadn't landed a job and didn't qualify for state aid. I don't know how he and his family survived, but at least he hadn't been hauled off to jail again, and now his song had been sung.

On our second to last night, the Soviet Peace Committee arranged a relaxing evening at a nightclub, but most of us wouldn't be there; we'd planned another foray into Moscow's forbidden suburbs, and our illicit numbers had climbed to eleven.

On the subway Yuri instructed: "Stay in twos and threes on different street corners. Hide cameras and jewelry. Don't look too Western." I looked disparagingly at my Nikes, which were not made in Novosibirsk.

Paul and Yuri disappeared down a dark alley and soon returned with a young man. "Where Americans?" he asked. Yuri discreetly nodded toward the four corners, after which his contact waved us in. "KGB arrest if want to."

Following him to an upscale neighborhood, I looked for a stakeout but never saw one. Instead we went to a comfortable flat where we talked with him and his wife, young professionals willing to take risks for human rights that we took for granted. They hoped to have kids one day and wanted them to grow up free.

Overly tired at breakfast the following morning, I was startled by a crushing bear hug from behind. Cool Sasha—our KGB babysitter who was so nicknamed because of his steel, gray-blue eyes—asked with an emotionless smile, "So, Carroll. Why were you not at dinner last night? All of those in attendance had a wonderful time."

I pictured eleven empty seats around a banquet table and avoided looking directly into his demon eyes. "Not feeling well," I muttered.

"Many of you were sick last night. An upset stomach or a

bad headache? A migraine I think you call it? I stopped by your room to see if you were okay."

I wasn't in my room! My knees became weak.

"Are you okay now?" he said with a smirk.

Flustered, I said nothing. My mouth had gone dry.

Sasha stared at me before turning to "chat" with another reprobate. It seems that Jamie had suffered the same stomach ailment. Few things rattled my roommate, but Sasha's penetrating glare stopped him in his tracks. I entertained unpleasant visions of a strip search and interrogation.

Sasha was the only Russian we'd met without a British accent; his inflections were more reminiscent of my Michigan cousins, Bart and David.

"Did you ever live in the United States?" Sarah asked, wondering how he'd learned such nondescript American English. "Maybe Chicago?"

"No, I learned it from a book," he glowered.

Now, we all know people don't learn accents from a book. But I knew better than to push the issue; this operative was not to be trifled with. They were unaccustomed to challenges by "naïve" religious folks who were hopelessly contaminated by "the opiate of the people." The Soviet Union could be a scary place.

After fifteen exhausting days, I was ready to head home. The westbound flight seemed longer until a delegate produced a harmonica—we killed time by singing songs like "Home on the Range." While not one nostalgic American had a dry eye, the Russians on the flight thought we were all crazy.

At Dulles International Airport, one of our team fell to his knees and kissed the ground in imitation of Pope John Paul II. A customs agent smiled and said, "Welcome back."

Kate greeted me with a strangling hug and nonstop kisses. During the ride to Gloyd, we shared a few stories about our two weeks apart. She related myriad details while I doled out one-word answers.

"So how was the weather? Is it windy in March like here?"

"Cold. And, yes."

"Was the food any good?"

"Okay."

"Did you meet any foxy women?" *A test to see if I was listening.*

"A few," I said with fake grin.

She kept her eyes on the road, but I saw her smirk.

"Sorry, Kate, I'm exhausted. For the last two weeks I've been speaking through interpreters. It gave me lag time to think."

"Okay. I'll do all the talking," she said. And for the entire forty-five minute ride, she did.

"Debbie and I got together and Eric came over ... Russell's been riding a lot and Tara's been busy with friends ... Joel often asked about you ... Mom had us over for dinner and ..."

I enjoyed every minute of it.

A month or so later, Kate was reading through my journal when she paused at a brief entry: *Can't get going. Tired of same BS. Lay in bed half the day*. She grabbed her diary, realizing that at that precise moment, when I was depressed in Moscow, she'd sensed something terribly wrong and wrote in her diary: *Urgent prayer needed for Carroll.* Across ten thousand miles and nine time zones, our spiritual connection had remained secure.

Somewhere in the dark recesses of the Russian Secret Service on Lubyanka Square, there's a file on Dr. Carroll James of Gloyd. I got chills thinking about that.

It was good to be back in the United States.

CHAPTER NINETEEN

A New Beginning

After I returned from Russia, Kate and I continued to build our yet unfinished home.

"It's gonna take twenty years to finish this place," Kate said with a chuckle as she rolled primer on the bedroom drywall. She was wrong; it would take longer.

As I considered all the time, energy, and money we were putting into our three-bedroom home, I felt a little guilty about the cramped Soviet flats.

"Why don't we get something smaller," I suggested at breakfast one day.

"Then where would you put that home office we talked about?" Kate said.

Knowing she was right, I drew up architectural plans for converting the garage into a dental office and proudly submitted them to the Park and Planning office. The county promptly rejected them.

The clerk I talked with used red ink to mark up my meticulous blueprints, which had taken me untold hours to draw to scale with a straightedge and T-square.

"Now redo them like this," he said, trying to be helpful.

It took me several more weeks, using his guidelines, but those plans were immediately rejected by another clerk. I submitted a third draft to a third gentleman who spoke little English but nevertheless stamped "Accepted" on them. I wished Dr. Lee had taught me how to say "Thank you" in Korean.

I hired a plumber and an electrician, while I served as the carpenter, and I eventually obtained an occupancy certificate, just as the money ran out. Like in my Rockville office, I made do with second-hand furnishings, cramming an old file cabinet and my childhood desk into a tiny alcove that served as a business office, while a worn-out couch from Frank's contact lens and artificial eye practice filled the small waiting room. Because the garage floor sloped to the outside, it angled downhill, making folks instinctively lean uphill. After unconsciously squirming in anticipation, they'd slowly drift south into their downside neighbor.

Pencils regularly rolled off the desk, which I thought was funny. Not Kate. "I'm forever picking them up off the floor," she growled. To keep the peace, I shimmed the two downhill legs with wooden blocks—but I found it less amusing when my instruments rolled across the bracket table, despite attempts by my supply man to level the second-hand dental chair. What's more, my stool, along with the assistant's, would subtly drift while we worked, as if possessed. I'd find myself stretching to reach the patient while my assistant crowded in from topside. It was all reminiscent of Dr. Frieden's office; I'd passed judgment on him too soon.

But my chief concern about this venture was its rural setting, which violated the three basic rules of business: location, location, and location. Gloyd sat atop a gentle knoll, an hour's drive northwest of Washington, DC. Its main street—the only street—doglegged to the left after paralleling the railroad tracks for a hundred yards. Victorian homes flanked a quarter mile of tar-and-chip road lined by ancient shade trees. Near the far end of town, the quaint 1878 church featured a tall steeple and picturesque graveyard; many of the gravestones were too weather-worn to read.

Pastor Winston, who sponsored my trip to Russia, lived in the manse across the street with his wife, son, and dog. Many men of the cloth could be identified by a collar or vestments. Not Winston. Dressed in overalls and work boots to blend with the country folk, he invited himself over shortly after we moved in. Plopping onto our couch, he smiled and said, "Welcome to Gloyd," then proceeded to describe a few of the more colorful characters around the area. "Your neighbor Harold is salt of the earth—will do anything for you. But don't cross his wife. She heads up the elders and runs the church with an iron hand."

"Yeah. We met him when our horse got loose and clobbered a car," I said sheepishly.

"I heard about that," he said.

Of course he had. Everyone knew everything about everyone in Gloyd.

"They say you're opening a dental office," he continued. "That should be interesting." No encouragement, but no discouragement either.

Kate and I liked Winston and decided to attend his church. After Sarah and I represented Gloyd in the USSR, the church's congregants reciprocated by supporting my new dental office.

Opening day arrived with only one patient, a young family man from the church. I cleaned his teeth and Kate assisted me with a filling. Although a little rusty, she managed to avoid blowing air up his nose. He smiled when he got up and said, "You're okay as far as dentists go!"

More gung-ho than ever, I posted a handmade flyer on the country store's community board. The advertisement was proudly displayed amongst scraps of paper that announced newborn pups; hay, straw, and grain for sale; sheep shearers, farriers, and welders; a brush hog and backhoe operator; chicks, goats, and rabbits for purchase; and free barn cats. Several faded shards of ruled paper gave directions to long-gone yard sales.

One day, an old-timer went in to buy a pouch of chaw, rubbed his sore jaw, copied my phone number, and called Kate. "Got a tooth been painin' me for some time."

"I've got an opening first thing tomorrow morning," she said, failing to mention that the doctor had no other appointments scheduled in Gloyd. He was happy that we could see him so quickly, and we were thrilled to "squeeze" him in.

He volunteered that he and his wife lived in a frame house next to the railroad tracks behind the country store. "Me an' the little woman lived in these parts fer years. Gloyd never had no dentist afore."

I had a hard time getting to sleep that night, anticipating that the next day might establish a solid reputation for me. I'd finally drifted off when a cacophony of howling dogs drifted in through the open bedroom windows. Kate looked at the clock on her nightstand and jumped out of bed. "Pipe down out there—it's two a.m.," she yelled through the screen before realizing that Rusty, our mongrel Irish setter, was making most of the racket.

I half opened my eyes and noticed streaks of reddish-orange flickering on the bedroom wall opposite the window.

Fire!

Bolting out of bed, I threw up the screen and stuck my head out to see if it was spreading our way, remembering our close call with fire on moving day.

"Do you think anyone's called the fire department?" I asked.

"Maybe. Shouldn't we get dressed just in case?" Kate suggested.

"I guess."

Mesmerized by the flickering glow that filtered through the not-too-distant trees, neither of us budged. It came from the direction of the town center, a half mile away, and Kate wanted to go investigate.

Not me. "If it gets any closer, wake me up," I said, crawling back under the sheets to get some rest before my morning appointment.

She reluctantly pulled herself away from the window and climbed in beside me. "I think it's pretty far away, anyway."

I rolled over and drifted off while fire engines wailed in the distance.

Six o'clock came early but Kate and I were already dressed and trudging sleepy-eyed toward town. Stabletown Road was clogged by commuters who sometimes took the back roads to avoid rush hour on I-270, but there was never anything like a traffic jam ... until that day.

"I'll bet last night's fire is responsible," Kate said as we walked past stalled cars and climbed the hill to the country store.

Cresting the summit, we saw the cause of the previous night's canine commotion: a freight train from Detroit had derailed, strewing scores of shiny new Cadillacs, along with several railroad cars, like matchbox cars. Trees were uprooted and telephone poles were knocked over.

Trapped in the impenetrable logjam, bewildered businessmen clutching their briefcases wandered aimlessly, waiting in vain for a train that wasn't coming, and a line had formed at the outdoor pay phone. It was so surreal that I almost expected to see Rod Serling leaning against the porch post, smoking a cigarette and describing the scene as taking place "somewhere in the Twilight Zone."

How was it that television crews always managed to elbow their way through the mess? Cameramen seemed to be everywhere.

Dressed in work boots, faded blue jeans, an old flannel shirt, and a battered baseball cap, I must've looked like the quintessential local yokel. Within minutes, a buxom, blond reporter shoved a microphone in my face while her cameraman aimed his video. She nodded and he flipped on his halogen spotlight, half-blinding me. Behind the unnatural radiance, the pretty commentator's disembodied voice asked me, "What's your name, sir?"

"Carroll," I mumbled, stuffing my hands into my torn pockets.

"Well, Daryl. What's your impression of last night's train wreck?"

"I heard something but was so tired, I just rolled over to get some sleep." Then I added, "And it's Carroll—two Rs and two Ls."

Apparently, my commentary wasn't riveting enough for fast-breaking, eyewitness news—the halogen light faded as the reporter yelled "cut" and went in search of a more promising bystander.

Kate boldly stepped forward with eight-month-old Joel on her hip. Reveling in the limelight, she was infinitely more articulate than I was. The correspondent asked several questions that Kate enthusiastically answered. As a result, she was showcased on the noon, six o'clock, and late-night news, all of which were dutifully recorded on our new VCR.

Thankfully, no one on the ill-fated train was injured, but an old farmhouse that sat hard by the tracks had been violently knocked off its stone foundation, landing in a shattered heap of wood and plasterboard on Gloyd's main street. Winston announced to the shell-shocked crowd that an elderly couple had been sleeping soundly on the second floor when it was struck. "They tumbled through the collapsing house and landed in the cellar," he said. "They're at the hospital but seem to be okay." Apparently they had numerous contusions and bruises, but no broken bones.

Kate and I gazed down into the exposed, debris-filled cellar before looking at the rubble trailing across the street. It was truly a miracle that the aged couple had escaped serious injury; angels had clearly watched over them on that fateful day. I tried to imagine the horror of being awakened by a deafening metallic screech while a train smashed into our house, then sent us plummeting two stories through the chaos. My worst nightmares could not compare.

Well, maybe that witch in Grandma's farmhouse came close.

While I stumbled through the wreckage, it dawned on me that the demolished house was once opposite the country store. The fog in my coffee-deprived brain slowly lifted as I questioned a Gloyd parishioner.

"So, Ginger. Who lives ... lived ... in that house?"

"The Shirleys."

"Bud Shirley?" I asked.

"Yep. Him and his wife, Dorothy," Ginger said with a sad look. "Poor folks. Could've been worse, though."

I stared blankly and turned introspective. *What I hoped would be my second patient is my first cancellation.* That was a selfish thought, but at any rate, Bud's toothache would have to wait.

Not only was I thankful that the Shirleys were okay, I was thankful for my family. With Kate's hand cradled in mine, we slowly walked home while the rising sun of a new day chased away the surrounding mist and warmed our souls.

I extracted Bud's tooth the following week and all went well. Afterward, he shared accolades with friends about a competent new dentist in Gloyd. Through fits and starts, neighbors slowly drifted into our office. It was a solid beginning.

CHAPTER TWENTY

A Tale of Two Offices

A rural home office might've seemed anachronistic in a time when healthcare trends were moving away from solo practices and more toward multidiscipline offices with a slew of hygienists and expanded duty auxiliaries. And while a home office was becoming as rare as rotary telephones, one in the rural countryside, despite its proximity to the encroaching suburban sprawl, was unheard of.

But it seemed like a perfect way to develop close ties with the community, and after our modest opening, we were soon rolling with Kate assuming the roles of receptionist, office manager, and assistant while I worked not only as the dentist but as the hygienist too. (In my Rockville office, I had a hygienist, Esther, who drove me crazy, a story related in book two, *The Whole Tooth.*) A fresh start without personality conflicts inherent in a larger staff was a chief goal in Gloyd. I also discovered unforeseen advantages to a home practice.

For one, I was always happy to treat a patient during off hours if it was a real emergency. No one can predict when little Johnny is going to fall off his bike and break a front tooth … or when that vague pain that's been around for a year suddenly develops into a full-blown abscess and hurts like crazy, keeping the person awake at night. Those folks needed to be seen right away, and I gladly came to the rescue.

Rockville patients, on the other hand, could sometimes push the envelope when it came to "emergencies." After driving forty-five minutes to care for a patient, I'd ask, "So which tooth is it and how long has it been bothering you?"

"The one in the back and it started Monday," the person might say.

"Has it kept you up at night?"

"Naw. It's not been that bad," he would say. "I just didn't want to use my sick leave," which was not what he told me on the phone when he sounded so desperate.

So you called me on a Saturday night? I'd think, fuming inside. After spending a few minutes smoothing off a little chip, I'd drive forty-five minutes back to Gloyd and sit down to a cold dinner that Kate would reheat in the microwave.

My home office was the solution to this madness. When folks called, I'd start giving them directions to Gloyd.

"Hop on I-270 until you get to the exit. Go west for four miles and then—"

Suddenly they would stop me, saying their problem could wait until Monday. If it was a true emergency, the person would drive out (often thinking they were lost when they passed the dairy farm and sawmill) and eventually find our home, especially if the pain was bad enough. I was happy to take care of them, especially with Kate available to assist me with more comprehensive treatment.

I really didn't mind seeing after-hours emergencies—it's part of the job—as long as I wasn't taken advantage of. And even though insurance companies would pay a higher rate for emergency visits, I never tacked on the extra fee; I liked my patients too much to hassle them with picayune stuff.

Once my practice had been open long enough for people in town to know about me (remember, word in a small town travels fast), we heard a knock on the front door one afternoon while eating Sunday dinner.

"I wonder who that could be?" I said. Nobody we knew used the front door.

A lean farmer in well-worn overalls and a straw hat asked, "You the dentist?"

"Yep," I replied.

"I got me a loose tooth here. Can't get it out and it's started painin' me."

"Okay," I said. "I'll meet you at the office door on the side by the parking lot."

While my family finished dinner, I pulled his tooth and returned in time for dessert. The farmer paid me from a dirty wad of cash and gave me a dozen eggs to boot. I've also received the likes of venison and other exotics from some of the locals (but I always declined goat cheese).

I soon discovered that a myriad of well-to-do folks lived upcountry. Through the Lions Club, the Country Club, our kids' schools, and our church, I met many suburbanites who had moved to escape the DC congestion: attorneys, professors, journalists, physicians, politicians, and even a couple of CIA analysts (who couldn't discuss exactly what they did).

The satellite office was like having two practices that were polar opposites, but in one location. Professionals and the needy rubbed elbows in the waiting room, especially intimate on that tilted couch. I performed state-of-the-art treatment on individuals requesting aesthetic work while carving out time to help indigent folks so they weren't forced to travel to charitable clinics umpteen miles away. It became more gratifying than I had ever imagined.

Not long after establishing the satellite office, I enrolled in graduate school for orthodontics so parents wouldn't have to schlep their kids to some distant location for their monthly appointments. After attaining that degree, entire families were often scheduled for two to three hours to complete everyone's periodic checkups and cleanings, adjustment of braces, and restorative work. Kate and I thoroughly enjoyed it when whole clans took over the office during after-school hours, and it helped especially large ones who had busy schedules.

Over time, Kate and I began to get a real feel for the community and its environs. A rural home office might have been an anachronism to some, but I wouldn't have traded it for a cold office in a strip mall or some medical building for anything. I already had that in Rockville, and though I cared equally for those patients, the feeling I had treating the hometown folk simply couldn't compare.

CHAPTER TWENTY-ONE

You Rang?

Over in Rockville, Dr. Dolph's cousin Herman followed me to Minor Medical when I left Rolph's to set up my own private practice. Rolph was incensed at me—and also at Herman—for leaving his practice. To save face, Rolph insisted that Herman return to his office as a patient: blood is thicker than water, right? Or so he thought.

A year later Herman was back at my practice.

"Frankly, Carroll," he said, "you're a better dentist. My cousin's place is a factory."

When—years later—I closed the Rockville office for good, he followed me to Gloyd, way out in the country.

Herman had served in the Pacific during WWII, where he learned to play the trumpet and other pop instruments. He returned home to a hero's welcome and formed a jazz band as a sideline to his government job as an analyst at the Patent Office. One Sunday afternoon, Kate and I went to watch him and his band perform in a park, and we took a friend along who brought a large cooler of beer and snacks, thinking we were going to see a miniature Woodstock. Instead, Herman's combo played all forties stuff: "Boogey-Woogey Bugle Boy," "Baby, It's Cold Outside," "In the Mood," and more. Although it was a little behind our time, the band was good, and all of us enjoyed it. Maybe it was the beer.

Though quite a character, Herman's perpetual grin exuded an inner warmth, and his wife was a sweetheart with a high-pitched cartoon voice similar to Minnie Mouse's. Like Herman, she had a big heart and I quickly learned to ignore her vocal patterns to focus on how genuine she was. Everyone in the office enjoyed their appointments.

Only once did I see Herman with the blues not of the musical variety—when his lovely wife of forty years passed away. Kate and I mourned the loss for all of us, and it took several years for Herman to move on. But at some point, he hooked up with a lady friend named Trixie who looked about his age. She couldn't understand why he drove from Bethesda to the middle of nowhere for a dental appointment, but he did, which was gratifying to me and the staff. It didn't take long, though, for Trixie to appreciate the trip: she loved chatting with Kate while Herman was back getting his teeth cleaned, so much so that she rarely got the chance to open the novel she'd brought along to kill time.

Getting on in years, Herman continued to drive when he should have stopped. Case in point: he once plowed into the hedge—with Trixie riding shotgun—at the top of our parking lot after mistaking the accelerator for the brake. Ramming a bush that was half-pushed over, he got the bumper entangled in it. Horrified, he threw the car in reverse and further shredded the bush as it tore away from under the front fender.

"Crap—this visit's gonna cost me a bundle," he mumbled as he came into the office. "I put a hole in your hedge, Kate. Sorry about that."

"Don't worry about the bushes, Herman. They'll grow back. Are you and your car okay?"

"I'm fine, it's fine. Just a few scratches that'll buff out," he said. "Except for the fender ... it's hanging kinda funny. Do you have any duct tape round here?" Being an ingenious WWII vet, he could fix anything with duct tape.

A couple years later, Herman suffered a heart attack, but he remained upbeat. Although he now shuffled along with the help of a cane, he tried to keep up with the times. His kids showed him how to use e-mail and then a cell phone. Like many patients, he would forget to turn his phone off despite the prominently posted sign: *No Cell Phones.*

Over the years, Herman's upper front teeth repeatedly fractured, and I brought them back to life with several patch jobs. It wasn't until he was eighty-four that he was forced by circumstances to do it right—which meant expensive crowns.

"My front teeth got whacked," he told Kate. "It was an accident." She was afraid to ask exactly what happened.

After he arrived he announced, "I gotta get 'em fixed right away. Trixie and I are leaving for her family reunion in two days."

Kate had squeezed him into a very busy schedule, but after examining him I realized that it would take a couple of hours to do the job properly.

"I'll make some temps that will look nice for the reunion," I offered. "Then we'll make permanent crowns after you get back."

"Whatever you say. You're the doc."

About halfway through the procedure, his phone rang. "I'm in the dental chair right now," Herman said. "No, he's almost done. I'll be there shortly."

"Was that Trixie on the line?" I asked.

"Yeah."

"You drove out here alone, Herman?"

"Yep. Trixie's at the hairdresser. Guess her beauty treatment doesn't take as long as my dental appointment," he said with a grin. "She's waiting for me to pick her up so we can pack for Austin."

That's scary. I didn't think he drove anymore, I thought, thinking of the bushes. "We'll have you outta here soon," I said, not wanting him to feel rushed, especially behind the wheel.

When he reached under his sweater to put his cell phone away, he somehow missed his shirt pocket and it fell, presumably inside his shirt.

"I'll find it later, Carroll," he told me. "Go ahead and finish up."

The temporary crowns were soon cemented in place and he was ready to go.

"Have a good trip, Herman," I said, patting him on the back. "Be easy on these temps so they don't fall off during the reunion. Don't eat anything hard or sticky."

He smiled and turned to leave.

We had become overly busy after squeezing Herman into our schedule, and I had to dash to examine the hygiene patient. My head was halfway within his distended maw when I heard Herman in the distance. "It must've fallen into the cushion."

I assumed he was talking about the misplaced cell phone.

"Uh, I don't see it," said Doreen, my young assistant who searched under, over, and around the dental chair Herman had just vacated. On her hands and knees, she looked up and announced, "I think it went down your shirt, Mr. Herman."

"I guess it must have," he said skeptically.

"I'm sorry, Mr. Herman. But I've got to clean this room now. Another patient is waiting."

Herman shuffled toward the overflowing waiting room with his cane and touring hat in hand to find that every seat, including the two stools in the kids' corner, was occupied. He leaned over the front desk. "Kate, can you help me check my clothes? I can't seem to find my cell phone anywhere."

She had overheard the unsuccessful search for his phone and suggested that maybe it slid between his shirt and sweater. "What's your number, Herman? I'll call it so we can hear it ring."

She dialed the given number. Someone answered, but it

wasn't Herman. She tried again. Another wrong number. On the third attempt, a muffled old rendition of "When the Saints Go Marching In" came from the region of his baggy pants.

Kate stepped out from behind the counter. "Let me take a look, Herman." She gently patted down his legs but stopped shy of the suspected location. No luck. She timidly felt around his empty back pockets, first one and then the other. One patient waiting announced, "You wouldn't make much of a TSA agent, Kate." Herman turned, smiled at the man, and playfully shook his butt. Kate declined to further explore.

The waiting room became a cheering section as everyone urged her to call him again.

"I think I hear it ringing down the other leg!"

"No, check his waist in the front, near his belt buckle."

Herman, discarding his cane in all the excitement, slowly turned around with his arms high in the air, putting on a show for everyone.

"Why don't you go into the bathroom and look for it?" Kate finally said.

A few minutes later, Herman yelled for Kate from the closed bathroom door.

"Try it now," he said as loudly as he could.

Through the door came his ringtone, then he stepped out, holding his pants in one hand, his bony legs supported by the cane he held in the other. "I still can't find it," he said, grinning.

Just then, the singing phone fell out of his skivvies and clacked to the floor. With the mystery solved, I bent over to retrieve it while Herman put his pants back on—right there in the bustling hallway for all to see. There wasn't a dry eye in the office from all the laughter.

Kate later confessed. "Somehow, I knew it was in his underwear. But I really didn't want to look that closely."

"Yep," I said playfully, "it was either there, or he's got a singing Willy."

The next day Kate went to the post office, where Pastor Winston was leisurely chatting with an attorney from Gloyd. Winston stopped in mid-sentence and excused himself. He then turned toward my wife. "Hey, Kate—can you give me a call?"

She tipped her head, confused. "Excuse me?"

"Seems I've misplaced my cell phone," he said, shaking his booty with a twinkle in his eye. Spinning around with his hands in the air, he asked, "How 'bout giving me a pat-down and checking my pockets, Kate?"

Apparently word of the incident had quickly spread throughout Gloyd.

Kate rushed out, embarrassed and laughing, completely forgetting the mail she came there for.

Postscript: Herman wore white jockeys, which were more functional to catch a falling cell phone than Dr. Frieden's polka dot boxers ever would've been.

CHAPTER TWENTY-TWO

From Russia with Hope

My Gloyd practice was fairly new when the Soviet Peace Committee sent a delegation to the United States in exchange for the one we sent to the USSR. In previous years, their teams comprised a handpicked elite, but the 1988 team included a steel worker, an elementary school teacher, a plumber, a carpenter, and two low-level managers. The quintessential KGB operative, thinly disguised as another teacher, was easily identified by his shifty eyes and arrogant bearing. And they were all still card-carrying Communists.

Unlike my group's sojourn in the USSR when we had to stay in a guarded hotel, the Soviet delegates of US-USSR Bridges for Peace were allowed to stay in private homes around the DC Beltway. The KGB guy boarded at St. Albans School as a guest of Jamie's (who never let him get away with any revisionist propaganda BS); two of the intelligentsia: a dentist, Yuri, and an economist, Leila, were proudly welcomed to the modest ranch home of Art, an elder at Pastor Winston's church, and his wife, Mary, a spitfire country girl.

Leila, who worked closely with President Gorbachev, was

an expert on North America's economy. Slender and of average height, with short brown hair and blue eyes, she was stylishly attired and very pretty (except for her severely crowded teeth—a dentist notices that sort of thing). Having traveled several times to the United States and Canada, she was well versed in Western customs.

Yuri, on the other hand, might've been mistaken for blue collar if not for his advanced degree and lofty title: Chairman of the Moscow University College of Dental Science. Middle-aged, he was tall and wiry with chaotic patches of thinning gray hair that never looked combed. His hesitant English smacked of a crash course.

Although their schedule was strictly controlled by the Soviet embassy, it did allow free time, and nothing was scheduled for Yuri and Leila's first day, giving them time to recover from jet lag.

"Hey, Art," I said. "Let's take them for a ride around the countryside."

The two delegates nodded in agreement.

Yuri took my proffered cowboy hat and hopped in the back of our pickup. Not wanting to look like a spoilsport, Leila climbed into the truck bed beside him (but refused to wear Kate's hat). Yuri grinned nonstop, bouncing through the countryside while Leila grimaced—maybe because her hair, even though short-ish, kept blowing in her eyes. The hat would've helped.

After the ride, and after Leila had cleared her throat of bugs, they spent the rest of the day roaming our farmette. Yuri wanted to ride a horse; he sat cockeyed and beamed while I led him around the field. Leila, a city-girl, merely tolerated Kate's horse. After dismounting, she spent a lot of time brushing horsehair off her clothes.

Yuri was a lover of antiques and was delighted when Art informed him that we had an antique store "right 'ere in town beside the country store." Although it was an easy walk to town, Yuri wanted to take another ride in the truck. Leila had had enough of dirty truck beds and stayed back at the house with Mary.

"Downtown" Gloyd was a motley assortment of old buildings: the antique shop, which used to be the train station; a country store run by Koreans who could almost speak English; an auto repair shop for American-made only (no metric tools); and the post office, which lacked a bathroom for Dosia, the postmaster and only postal employee other than Art. A cardboard sign that read "Back in Fifteen Minutes" on the counter meant she'd gone home to take care of necessary business.

With great expectations, Yuri strode confidently into the antique shop, greeted by the jingle of a bell on the door. But his smile soon faded as he picked up an old farm implement or some other knickknack, studied it for a second, then put it down, frowning.

"Where antiques?" He said.

"Everything in here is an antique, Yuri," I replied.

He looked at me sideways. "Just old junk."

From where he stood, he was right; in Europe, antiques can be many centuries old. Disappointed, we soon left the store.

A couple days later, we ventured into the nearby suburbs—in my car, not the truck. Leila shook her head in disbelief at the neat, modern homes.

"This is just a showcase to impress us," she said with a huff.

Cosmopolitan Leila, only familiar with the glitter around US convention centers and convinced that destitution reigned everywhere else, probably thought the neighborhood was our version of a Potemkin village.

"Yes. There's poverty and homelessness—more than we'd like—but not everywhere," I tried to explain. "My grandparents were extremely poor, even by American standards. But even then there were opportunities, such that I could become a doctor."

"You are a rich dentist," Leila said adamantly. "Most Americans live in squalor."

"Actually, most are middle class. It's true that some are filthy rich and some are dirt poor. But those are extremes."

"Not so. We have newsreels, show homeless peoples everywhere. You just show best," said Yuri. It was one of the few times over their two-week stay that he allied himself with Leila. Prejudices, fueled by a closely manipulated media, were hard to dispel.

"How about this?" I proposed. "We'll go anywhere you like. You just tell me when and where to turn the car."

My offer seemed to intrigue Yuri. *What if the capitalist isn't bluffing*, his eyes seemed to ask.

Although Kate and I own a few acres, our house is an average size, bigger than some, smaller than many. But to the Russians it seemed palatial. Not only that, but any dog, but especially a big one, was a status symbol in Russia. And we had three: two rambunctious litter mates and the patriarch, Rusty. Leila squealed with delight when they jumped on the couch to snuggle with her. Yuri, however, thought we were just showing off.

"Many peoples—families—live here?" Yuri had asked the first day.

"Just me, Kate, and the three kids," I said.

They looked incredulous. After visiting my mom's townhouse ("No, she doesn't live with us.") and my brother's Pyleton home ("Neither does his family."), it slowly dawned on them that we might actually be telling the truth.

Their second week in the States, we were touring DC when I got lost—which is not hard to do in Washington, even for natives—and we inadvertently wandered into a neighborhood of ramshackle homes, with seedy-looking people sitting idly on the decaying front stoops. Bored youths hung out on street corners, and I quietly locked the car doors.

"This is one of the poorer sections of town, so you take precautions," I explained.

Leila chimed in from the backseat. "This is exactly what we see on our news. It's everywhere."

"Our media also focuses on America's crime and social problems, which helps us correct them," I countered. "But it's not everywhere ... I'll still go wherever you want to."

Although they seemed puzzled at how open I was, I think the wall of distrust was slowly crumbling.

Leila, her reverie broken, then spoke up. "Can we go to a K-Mart?"

"Yes, I hear of K-Mart," Yuri enthusiastically echoed.

I stifled a laugh and agreed with a shrug.

On a sunny afternoon, before a scheduled conference at Hood College, we stopped at the Frederick K-Mart megastore to experience its "magic." The two Russkies wandered around like kids in a toy store. Yuri's mouth stood agape as he eyed the variety and quantity of goods on display. Even Leila seemed overwhelmed, having never seen anything like it; there weren't many big-box stores near the plush downtown hotels where she normally stayed.

It all suggested that Soviet media reports of endless shortages in the West might not be completely true. The novel *1984* came to mind: "If the lie is big enough and repeated often enough, the masses will eventually believe it."

Despite the marvel they were experiencing, however, nothing compared to the sporting goods section, where they were taken aback by the myriad guns for sale.

"Anyone buy?" Yuri queried.

"Most folks. There are background checks for criminal records and they're age-restricted. But it's kind of loose and if nothing is found in short order, then yes, anyone can buy a gun."

"People in America can shoot anyone they want to," Leila calmly told Yuri.

"It does happen and too often," I said. "It's one of many problems we're trying to work out. But we do it openly."

They weren't buying it, so I changed tacks.

"I was captain of my high school rifle team when we won

the state championship," I said, grinning proudly, explaining how we used targets. "I can show you my target rifle when we get back to the house."

"*Nyet*," they nervously exclaimed in unison.

After a thorough walk-through, Leila wasn't interested in buying anything; as a privileged apparatchik, she could get goods unavailable to other Russians in Moscow. Yuri, on the other hand, was taking a lot of pictures and announced that he needed AA batteries for his camera.

I looked at the checkout line. "I think it will take too long. We're due at Hood soon. I've got extra batteries you can have at the house."

"*Nyet*. I buy myself," said Yuri.

Long lines were nothing to him; he was used to waiting hours for a stale loaf of bread or fatty slab of beef. In comparison, the K-Mart line was moving pretty fast, so I conceded.

When we got to the register, Yuri looked dumbfounded at the pimple-faced, gum-chewing young girl with orange and green hair. When he finally placed the shrink-wrapped AAs on the conveyer belt, she yawned, blew a bubble, and scanned the bar code. "That'll be three dollars and fourteen cents," she mumbled.

Carefully gauging the adolescent's immaturity, he straightened up to appear even taller than he was. He squinted menacingly at the chubby little thing, then boomed with authority, "I give two dollars!"

"Huh … what?" The no-longer-bored cashier stopped twirling her hair and repeated, "That's three dollars and fourteen cents with tax."

"*Nyet* … No! Two dollar fifty cents. Final offer!"

Flustered, she lightly stomped one foot and stammered, "I … I can't do that mister. It's three dollars and fourteen cents."

All ambient chattering ceased as other shoppers craned their necks to see what was going on.

Not to be dissuaded, Yuri raised his chin with a haughty air and loudly demanded, "I want speak owner."

That gave me pause. *So, just who is the* owner *of K-Mart?* Leaning toward me, Leila whispered, "Are American Jews like this?" Flabbergasted, I said nothing. I didn't even know Yuri was Jewish—never thought about it. Obviously, bigotry had not been eliminated in the worker's paradise any more than it had been in America.

The young gal shrugged her shoulders, re-scanned the package, and pointed at the computer screen. She looked desperate, her eyes pleading for anyone to help.

In an attempt to come to her aid, I said, "I have money, Yuri. I'll be glad to—"

He cut me short with an aristocratic wave, glared at the teen, and said through gritted teeth, "Let me speak boss. He know two dollars fifty cents good price."

As the line grew ever longer, and folks more irritated, Kate spoke up.

"We'll pay the difference, Yuri."

Maybe embarrassed by an offer from a woman, he slammed a five-spot on the counter. While impatient shoppers looked on from behind, he carefully counted his change—twice.

More livid than embarrassed, Leila refused to interpret for him at the Hood meeting, which was a big problem for Yuri whose English was poor at best. *I'm glad she didn't buy one of those guns,* I thought.

Toward the end of their visit, Yuri asked if he could see me in action as an American dentist. Although Leila had no desire to hang out in a dental office, she came along. Maybe she felt bad about shunning Yuri at the college, but while he was bent over my shoulder to watch me work, she fidgeted, paced, and begrudgingly translated.

"Most of our restorations are bonded," I explained. "Anterior crowns are all porcelain so they look nice. Kate has a couple up front."

"I like see," said Yuri, who had gold fillings that showed near the front of his mouth.

"Okay. I'll get Kate when she's not busy at the desk."

Yuri dug through his coat pockets and found a small plastic box that contained several Soviet drills and cutting disks. I looked carefully at them; the shafts weren't exactly straight and the holes in the disks weren't centered. *These things probably cut with the steadiness of a flat tire*, I thought, but didn't say. He was very proud of them.

"Do you mind letting Yuri see your Dicor crowns?" I asked Kate, showing her his drill collection.

"Sure," she said. But her skeptical smile said *No*. Kate half opened her mouth and whispered to me, "Only give him a mirror. Nothing sharp!"

Yuri seemed moderately impressed but said little.

Yuri and Leila's two-week visit was scheduled to end a couple weeks before Thanksgiving, so Gloyd Presbyterian decided to celebrate with an old-fashioned turkey dinner. Even though it was a little early for the holiday, it would be a fun send-off. So Kate and I crammed the quintessential card tables, TV trays, and folding chairs into our unfurnished living room (one table covered up the grease spot left on the rug from Halfway Dick's motorcycle), and about thirty neighbors squeezed in.

Before blessing the meal, Pastor Winston related a brief history of this American tradition:

> "In the darkest days of the American Civil War, President Abraham Lincoln called for a National Day of Thanksgiving to remember our many blessings. It was a

time when Americans were killing each other by the hundreds of thousands, yet he felt it appropriate to give thanks to our Creator, who should be remembered during the bad times as well as the good."

Leila and Yuri listened intently and respectfully bowed their heads during grace. Our small rural community had made an impression about the true source of America's ideals; we would also do well to remember, as President Lincoln had wished. Thanksgiving was the perfect ending for this visit from our Soviet guests.

Not long after Yuri and Leila's return to the USSR, the entrenched Russian dictatorship began the unprecedented process of peacefully dismantling itself. Communism simply does not work.

The Berlin Wall fell.

The Sunday following that momentous occasion, Pastor Winston commented on our historical exchange with the soon-to-be-former Soviet Union. He humbly complimented the congregation on successfully hosting its two citizen delegates, saying, "I'd like to believe that our little country church was responsible for taking one or two bricks out of that terrible wall."

I was thankful for the opportunity to have played a tiny role in that.

EPILOGUE

A simple brown envelope landed on my desk one day about a year after the Russians had left. I usually toss bulk-rate mail into the trash bin, but for some reason, I opened it. It promised exciting journeys to do dental work in rugged, poorly chartered regions around the world. Not long after I got that envelope, one life-changing mission proved nearly fatal ...

Uh oh ... gotta go. Rusty, our vagabond canine, just threw up an entire, partly digested groundhog on our bedroom carpet. So much for not allowing animals inside the house.

IN MEMORIAM

I wish to mention my good friends George and Ann, whose home we purchased in Pyleton, and whom Kate and I bowled with for years. A few years after we moved in, George was killed in a tragic road-rage incident. He was one of two innocent commuters who died on the way to work, along with one of the perpetrators; the other is still behind bars in a case that became nationally infamous. But the awareness that grew from the case didn't come in time for George and his family. He and Ann were deeply in love, and she never remarried.

George is sorely missed by all whose lives he touched.

STAY TUNED

My second book, *The Whole Tooth*, continues the Tooth Is Stranger Than Fiction series with more anecdotes, and more flashbacks to my Nealy Ridge childhood that will further explain why I had a burning desire to employ my dental skills in overseas missions. Folks in the many lost-in-time villages in which I have served were incredibly similar to my maternal family and their neighbors up on The Ridge—superficial differences in appearance and cultural traditions were unimportant to those seeking out a harsh existence from the land.

As both of my practices grew, I also hired more employees, some wonderfully efficient, some a lot of fun, and some just plain weird (I especially like talking about the weird ones)—and not just employees, but patients and friends as well. Periodically, some wacky individual would drift through my door, office, or otherwise, and lend me a great tale. In short, my country practice in Gloyd—surrounded by livestock, freely roaming pets, and stray varmints—nicely sets the stage for many more bizarre stories.

ACKNOWLEDGMENTS

Over fifty years in the making, this book depicts a life that has been a joy to experience. That's not to say it's all been fun—it hasn't. But the valleys, combined with peaks, have always made it worthwhile, and it would not have been so without family and the many friends who accompanied me along the way. I trust that none have been offended by my retelling—I wouldn't have included those zany capers if I didn't think so highly of the folks acting them out.

My lovely wife has been a loyal companion throughout this journey. As my constant anchor and most honest critic, she encouraged me to write these stories while actively discouraging me from relating others for the sake of propriety. Her dedication during the many hours I was absent in spirit is an example of true devotion. I'm more in love now than when we started.

Kudos to our kids who persevered through one strange childhood. These tales would not have been possible without them. I read several rough drafts out loud, even when they didn't want to listen, and they usually made faces, accompanied by, "Daaaad, you're not really going to write about *that*, are you?"

I coerced several friends into reading my early meanderings, and they had to wade through some pretty murky waters. I sincerely appreciate the perseverance of the following fine folks: Harriet, Stan, Steve, Pat, Susan, Wendy, and Gail.

My editors had not only many things to change in the way of punctuation and spelling, but also in clarity of thought and sentence structure. I can almost hear a groan as they realized that I don't know the difference between a winch—a rotary cable device—or a wench, a lady of the evening. Oops, spellcheck doesn't pick up everything.

Kudos to the editor of this second edition, who also edited my second book, *The Whole Tooth*. I deeply appreciate Stacey Aaronson's diligence and tolerance of my ramblings. She has been a joy to work with.

I offer my eternal thanks to everyone who has entered my life to make it what it is today and what it will be tomorrow. Not only this book, but also my chaotic journey would not have been possible without them.

And finally, but really foremost, to my Creator with whom all things are possible.

ABOUT THE AUTHOR

DR. CARROLL JAMES is a graduate of Gettysburg College, receiving his doctorate from the Farleigh-Dickenson University College of Dentistry in 1975. For two years, he practiced as an Associate in Rockville, MD, before establishing a private practice near Bethesda. After fifteen years in private practice, he began a satellite practice in Pyleton, MD (a fictional town). When that venture was unexpectedly interrupted, he purchased a home in the nearby rural town of Gloyd (also fictional), in which he established another satellite practice. That office grew exponentially and after another ten years, he moved from Rockville altogether and now enjoys treating patients in Gloyd.

Over the course of his career he has contributed articles to health columns, been published in the *CMDS Journal*, edited a monthly newsletter, lectured to medical students, written a blog, and contributed to the Academy of General Dentistry journal *Impact*. In addition, he and his family were featured in a human interest TV documentary about his wife's almost-fatal adventure in the jungles of southern Mexico.

As a child, Dr. James spent summers at his maternal grandparent's primitive home in the rugged Appalachian heartland of southwest Virginia. This experience forged his passion for serving impoverished peoples throughout the far reaches of the world.

Blessed with three children and four live-wire grandchildren, Carroll and his wife, Kate, continue to maintain their valued practice in their rural home.

59774551R00123

Made in the USA
Charleston, SC
13 August 2016